HIBERNIAN FC
On This Day

HIBERNIAN FC
On This Day

*History, Facts & Figures
from Every Day of the Year*

IAN COLQUHOUN & BOBBY SINNET

HIBERNIAN FC
On This Day
History, Facts & Figures from Every Day of the Year

All statistics, facts and figures are correct as of 1st August 2015

© Ian Colquhoun and Bobby Sinnet

Ian Colquhoun and Bobby Sinnet have asserted their rights in accordance with the Copyright, Designs and Patents Act 1988 to be identified as the authors of this work.

Published By:
Pitch Publishing (Brighton) Ltd
A2 Yeoman Gate
Yeoman Way
Durrington
BN13 3QZ

Email: info@pitchpublishing.co.uk
Web: www.pitchpublishing.co.uk

Published 2015

A catalogue record for this book is available from the British Library

ISBN 9781785310782

Typesetting and origination by Pitch Publishing
Printed in Great Britain by TJ International

DEDICATION

For Cameron (BS)

FOREWORD

Tom McManus played for Hibernian 129 times between 1999-2004, scoring 23 first-team goals. Signed in 1997 as an 'S' form, he scored some memorable goals for Hibs, including a stunning volley at Ibrox in 2003, a last-minute Scottish Cup tie 'winner ' at Rugby Park in 2001 and in a thrilling 2-2 draw with Everton at Easter Road in 2002, a game where a certain Alan Stubbs was playing at the back for Everton and in which a certain youngster named Wayne Rooney opened the scoring.

"I was lucky enough to play for Hibs for eight great years, during that time I played for the club as a youth, in the old Division One, the SPL, the domestic cups and the UEFA Cup. I am proud to have worn the green jersey. If you're a Hibby, I'm sure you'll love this book. Though this book contains stories regarding all eras in Hibernian's history, its writers deliberately chose to focus more on matches and events that are within living memory, so that there is more chance the reader can digest a snippet and think 'I was there' or 'I remember someone told me about that'. The beauty of this fun format of book is that it suits both the casual reader and the serious bookworm alike. It can be read aloud with family or friends, probably triggering some 'juicy' debates and reminiscences, or it can be read in one go, allowing the reader to immerse themselves in Hibernian's past, going from decade to decade, stadium to stadium, triumph to despair, all in one or a few sittings. Whether the reader is a regular who never misses a game or simply a keen fan who goes whenever they can, there's something in this book for every Hibs fan. It's by no means an in-depth study of one particular era or player/manager, but that more in-depth aspect is already catered for in the multitude of other books about the club by other good Hibby authors. What this book is, is an entertaining, thought provoking, easily accessible work that will grab the reader and won't let go, taking them on a kaleidoscopic journey through the past trials, triumphs and tribulations of Hibernian Football Club – The pride of Edinburgh. Ladies and gentlemen, here it is - *Hibernian FC : On This Day...*"

Tom McManus

INTRODUCTION

Happy 140th Birthday to Hibernian! It's our pleasure, as authors, to present you with this written kaleidoscope of some of the most memorable moments in Hibs' history. We hope that you enjoy reading it as much as we did writing it. Both of us have been watching Hibs for 60 years between us, so we've been researchers for most of our lives and it's a privilege to write about the club we love, for fellow fans of the club we love. What you are about to read is prologue...

Ian

I first attended Easter Road in 1986, our 4-1 home win against Chelsea on a hot summer evening, and asides a year in hospital, I've been a regular at Easter Road ever since. Hibs are in my blood, as they are in yours. Writing and researching this wee book with Bobby has been, for me, like time-travelling through Hibernian's past, an emotional journey, like 'Dr Who' but without the dodgy coat. It's been fascinating – one minute you're standing on the open East Terrace watching Turnbull's Tornadoes thrash Sporting Lisbon 6-1, the next you're on the rain-soaked Gorgie Road end terrace at Tynecastle as Steve Archibald beats Henry Smith to shatter a hoodoo, next you're back under the covered East Stand singing 'Sunshine On Leith' against AEK Athens, then you're sitting in the new East Stand as David Gray's screamer smashes into the top corner, silencing the Rangers fans. I hope the day by day journey is as fascinating and emotive for you, the reader – Hail Hail The Hibs Are Here, All For Goals And Glory Now...

Bobby

I first attended Easter Road in 1985, it was an end of season game against Rangers which Hibs won through a Paul Kane goal. Ever since I've been hooked, and for the last decade or so I've spent a considerable amount of time researching the complete History of Hibs which has been a labour of love. It's never easy being a Hibs fan, but there are always better days around the corner. It's not the despair. I can cope with the despair. It's the hope I can't stand.

@ihibs

ACKNOWLEDGEMENTS

My co-author, Bobby Sinnet, a true Hibby, without whom this book would have taken years to compile, and been nowhere near as fun to research. Also big shout outs to Garry O'Hagan, the good people at Hibeesbounce.com, Chris Kelly, my mum and dad Bette and John Colquhoun, Uncle Ronnie, Davie 'Disco' McDermott and Tony 'the fish' Divers, miscelleanous friends, fans and family who've encouraged me over the years , too many to mention. Thank You and God bless you. (IC)

I'd like to thank my co-author first of all – without Ian this book would never have happened. His drive and determination made sure I finished the part that I did. I'd also like to thank David Ross ex of www.scottishleague.net and his successor Alan Brown who both provided me with a wealth of help and information, and without them I'd never have written a book, period. I'd like to thank my wife for her patience and understanding and also my brother Andy and Lee Boyle who I've managed to watch a fair amount of football with over the years despite not sharing my allegiance. Special thanks to Mark Atkinson of the *Evening News* for sourcing some great photos and the *Evening News* for allowing them to be published.

Special thanks to Hibs legend Tom McManus for the foreword.

HIBERNIAN FC
On This Day

JANUARY

MONDAY 1st JANUARY 1973

Having recently won the cup and having hammered luckless Ayr United 8-0, Hibs travelled to Tynecastle for the New Year Edinburgh Derby. The high-flying Easter Road men were too strong for the Jambos and were 5-0 up by half-time, eventually running out 7-0 winners with goals from Alex Cropley and a brace apiece by Arthur Duncan, Jimmy O'Rourke and Alan Gordon. The match has gone down in Hibs folklore as simply 'The Greatest Game In History', and to this day remains Hearts' record home defeat. (It was equalled in 2013, when Celtic humiliated Hearts at Tynecastle by the same scoreline in The Scottish Cup, but Hibs' 1973 'demolition job' remains Hearts' record league defeat).

MONDAY 1st JANUARY 1996

Having just been mauled 0-7 at Ibrox a few days earlier, Hibs faced Hearts at Easter Road in the traditional new-year fixture. Hearts fans were predicting another thrashing for Alex Miller's men, and it looked on the cards when Neil Pointon gave Hearts an early lead. Hearts' Swedish striker Hans Eskilsson then missed an open-goal, later blaming noisy Hibs fans for his miss, saying they 'put him off'. Hibs fought back to win the game 2-1, thanks to superb goals by Kevin Harper and Michael O'Neil. The perfect reaction to the earlier mauling at Ibrox.

THURSDAY 1st JANUARY 1998

Struggling Hibs made the trip across the city to Tynecastle to play Hearts, who were 2-0 up inside the first ten-minutes, thanks to a brace from Steve Fulton, much to the delight of the home fans. Against all expectations, Jim Duffy's Hibs side came out fighting in the second half, and earned a 2-2 draw thanks to goals from Pat McGinlay and veteran striker Andy Walker. On the day, it was a good result, but to this day many Hibbies think that this 'lucky escape' bought the failing Duffy an extra few weeks in the Easter Road hot-seat, and thus contributed to Hibernian's relegation that season.

THURSDAY 2nd JANUARY 2003

Hibs and Hearts played out a remarkable 4-4 draw in the New Year Derby at Tynecastle. Hibs' Ian Murray had a design shaved into the hair on his head to celebrate the 30th anniversary of Hibs' 7-0 win at Tynecastle in 1973. Hibs were 2-0 up inside 17 minutes thanks to goals from Derek Townsley and Tam McManus, but Hearts were level by the 60 minute mark, thanks to a dodgy penalty and a strike by Mark De Vries. On loan Craig James put Hibs back in front, before Grant Brebner made it 4-2 to Hibs in injury time, after he had scored the rebound from a saved Paatelainen penalty. Graeme Weir bagged two injury time goals for Hearts to ensure the game finished 4-4. Normally, 4-4 at Tynecastle would be a good result, but the sequence of the scoring made it feel like two points dropped to most Hibs fans. Delighted Jambos behaved as if they had just won the Champions League.

SATURDAY 3rd JANUARY 2004

Partick Thistle made the trip along the M8 to play Bobby Williamson's side at Easter Road, in front of just over 8,000 fans. Hibs won the match 3-2, with goals from Stephen Dobbie and Garry O'Connor before half-time. The Jags fought back superbly after the interval and levelled the thrilling match at 2-2, until Steven Whittaker bagged the winner with just six minutes remaining, Hibs, somewhat luckily, collecting all three points.

WEDNESDAY 4th JANUARY 1989

Nearly 30,000 fans packed Easter Road for the New Year Derby. Hibs won 1-0 thanks to a strike by Eddie May. It was to be Hibs' last win over the Jambos until August 1994.

SATURDAY 4th JANUARY 1992

Alex Miller's men took on relegation-threatened Dunfermline in the clubs' fourth meeting of the season, the previous three, including the League Cup Final, having been won by the Hibees. Hibs made it four wins from four games against the Pars by thrashing the Fifers 5-0, goals coming from Mickey Weir, Gareth Evans and a hat-trick by Keith Wright, who was fast becoming Dunfermline's nemesis. The fifth and final meeting between the teams that season ended 0-0. Dunfermline were relegated at the end of the season.

SATURDAY 5th JANUARY 1952

In front of 23,000 fans at Easter Road, Hibs routed Stirling Albion by 8-0. There were hat-tricks for Lawrie Reilly and Bobby Combe, who was standing in for the injured Willie Ormond. Eddie Turnbull chipped in with the other two. The result cemented Hibs' position at the top of the Scottish Division One – a place they were to hold onto until the end of the season.

SATURDAY 6th JANUARY 1912

Dan McMichael's side recorded a fine victory, crushing Rangers 5-0 at home with 13,000 in attendance. George Rae (2), Adam Bell (2) and Harry Anderson were Hibs' scorers. Jimmy Hendren, a relative of centenary captain Pat Stanton played as a forward for Hibs, who were to finish the season in lowly 13th place whilst Rangers won the league.

SATURDAY 7th JANUARY 1984

Fewer than 5,000 supporters braved the freezing weather to see Hibernian play out a 1-1 draw with St Mirren. Graeme Harvey scored for the Hibees, who weren't enjoying the best of seasons under manager Pat Stanton, despite a good first few months of the campaign.

SATURDAY 8th JANUARY 1966

Greenock Morton were the visitors to Easter Road for a league match, back in the days when teams in the top flight only played each other twice a season. Bob Shankly's Hibernian side thrashed the 'Ton 4-1, Hibs' goals coming courtesy of a brace apiece from Jimmy O'Rourke and Peter Cormack. Due to also playing Morton home and away in the League Cup that season, Hibs had thus hammered luckless Morton four times, 5-1 at home in the other league match and winning 3-2 and 4-2 in the two League Cup group games.

SATURDAY 9th JANUARY 2010

John Hughes' Hibs side welcomed Scottish Junior League opponents Irvine Meadow to Easter Road in round four of the Scottish Cup. Hibernian won the match 3-0, leading 2-0 at half-time thanks to goals from Derek Riordan and Zemmama, before

Paul Hanlon scored the game's third and final goal just after 60 mins. The Junior side gave a good account of themselves and gave Hibs' 'keeper Graeme Smith a busy afternoon. This was the first time that a team from the Junior set-up had played a top-flight club in the Scottish Cup.

WEDNESDAY 10th JANUARY 1968

Over 40,000 fans were at Easter Road to see the second leg of Hibs UEFA Cup third round tie between Hibs and Leeds, the Yorkshiremen leading 1-0 from the 1st leg. Hibs took an early lead through Colin Stein, who'd had a goal chopped off in the first leg. The tie was headed for extra-time until the 87th minute, when Hibs 'keeper Willie Wilson gave away an indirect free-kick for breaking the 'four steps rule'. Leeds chipped the free-kick to Jack Charlton who equalised with a header, to knock Hibs out, 1-2 on aggregate. Had Hibs qualified for the quarter-finals, they would have joined Rangers and Dundee in the draw.

SATURDAY 11th JANUARY 1902

Hibs opened their Scottish Cup Campaign for the season with 2,000 people in attendance at Easter Road against Clyde. Billy McCartney and Johnny Divers scored Hibs' goals for Dan McMichael's side.

SATURDAY 12th JANUARY 1985

18,000 fans at Ibrox saw John Blackley's Hibs take on Rangers. The Hibees won the match 2-1, Hibs' goals coming from Brian Rice and from substitute Colin Harris. This was the Hibees' first win in 12 games, and their first victory over the 'Gers in 19 attempts, the last one having come back in 1979.

SATURDAY 13th JANUARY 1926

Hibs cruised to a comfortable victory against Greenock Morton in front of 8,000 fans at Easter Road. Jimmy McColl, the first player to score one hundred league goals for Hibs, chipped in with a double whilst John Walker and Harry Ritchie also netted in a 4-1 victory for Hibs. Jimmy Dunn, who was later to find fame as a Wembley Wizard, played for Hibs as did Hugh Shaw who was to manage the title winning teams in the 1950s.

SATURDAY 14th JANUARY 1928

Hibs visited West Lothian to play Bo'ness on league business, and a solitary goal by Jimmy Dunn, who would later star for Everton, took the points back to Edinburgh for Bobby Templeton's side. Bo'ness were to disappear from the senior game in 1933 and senior football only returned to West Lothian when Livingston took over Meadowbank Thistle in 1995.

WEDNESDAY 15th JANUARY 1969

Round three of the Fairs Cup saw Hibernian square-off against German cracks SV Hamburg at Easter Road in a second leg tie. Hibs had lost the first leg 1-0 in Germany. Despite having two goals disallowed and missing a penalty, Hibs won the game in Edinburgh 2-1 thanks to a Joe McBride double, but Uwe Seeler's goal at Easter Road meant that the tie finished 2-2 on aggregate, Hibs going out on the new away-goals rule. There were 27,000 fans at Easter Road for the second leg. Hibs had eliminated Lokomotive Leipzig of East Germany in the previous round, 4-1 on aggregate, and in the round before that had beaten Yugoslavian side Olimpija Ljubljana 5-1 over the two legs.

SATURDAY 16th JANUARY 1897

Hibernian met St Mirren for the first time this season, after their previous two scheduled encounters had been postponed. The Edinburgh side proved to be too strong for their mid-table rivals and chalked up a three goal victory to cement their position at the top of the Scottish League. In front of 4,000 fans, Barney Breslin, William Smith and George Dougal scored. The teams were to meet again a fortnight later, and this time St Mirren prevailed. This was to prove costly for Hibs; victory in that game would have seen them win the league.

SATURDAY 17th JANUARY 1931

On this day, the Scottish Cup first-round proper commenced and Hibs, managed by Bobby Templeton, were rewarded with a home tie against St. Cuthberts Wanderers, who were named after the patron saint of Kircudbright, where they were from. The non-league side restricted Hibs to a 3-1 victory and *The Scotsman* reported: "The

HIBS ON LEAGUE BUSINESS IN WEST LOTHIAN

Hibernians took little credit out of their match, they were the better side, yet so weak was their forward line, that the Wanderers' defence always seemed to have something in hand." It was the 75th minute before Hibs equalised a first half goal from Pagan, and went on to run out 3-1 winners.

THURSDAY 18th JANUARY 2007

Having drawn 2-2 in Aberdeen at the first attempt, John Collins' Hibs team faced a Scottish Cup third round replay against the 'Dons at Easter Road. Aberdeen took an early lead through Barry Nicholson but a sweet Steven Fletcher header and a superbly taken Michael Stewart volley had Hibs 2-1 up at the break. Abdessalam Benjelloun, more commonly known as 'Benji', was brought on at half-time and the substitution proved a masterstroke, as the striker bagged two goals within 11 minutes of coming on. It finished Hibs 4 Aberdeen 1.

SATURDAY 19th JANUARY 1952

Hibs retained top spot of the Scottish League with a 2-1 victory at Firhill against Partick Thistle. They extended their lead over Hearts to three points after their Edinburgh rivals drew at Tynecastle against Rangers. On their way to winning the league, Hibs took a first half lead through Bobby Combe, who was deputising for Willie Ormond on the left wing. Thistle equalised through Walker, before Hibs sealed the points with five minutes to go – earlier goalscorer Combe crossed for Archie Buchanan to head to the winner.

SATURDAY 20th JANUARY 1934

Bobby Templeton's Hibs side commenced their Scottish campaign in a truly remarkable game at Easter Road in front of 16,426 spectators. Hibs eventually prevailed as victors by 5-4 after being behind by 4-1 at the half-time break. Clyde had been dominant in the first half and Hibs' solitary goal by Rab Walls had occurred when Hibs were reduced in numbers by an injury to Malloy, who later returned to the action. In the second half Clyde sat back and allowed Hibs to attack and second half goals from Rab Walls, James Malloy and a double by recent signing from Hearts John Smith saw Hibs home. The takings from the game amounted to £659, excluding stand and tax.

SATURDAY 21st JANUARY 1911

In disagreeable weather at Cappielow, Hibs and Greenock Morton played out a 2-2 draw as the season moved towards a conclusion and both sides settled for the safety of mid table, in front of a respectable attendance of 7,000. Hibs took the lead twice in the match, first from David Anderson, and secondly through stalwart Matthew Patterson with a penalty. Morton equalised with goals from Gracie and May. Morton pressed for a winner, but the crossbar and the uprights came to the rescue of the Hibs goalkeeper Willie Allan. Full-back Peter Kerr was in his first full season for Hibs – he was to go on to play 483 League and Scottish Cup games.

SATURDAY 22nd JANUARY 1972

Pat Stanton missed a penalty for Eddie Turnbull's men in this league match at home to Motherwell. Hibs lost the match 2-1, Billy McEwan scoring for the 'Cabbage'. This match is notable as it was forward Alan Gordon's debut for Hibs. Gordon went on to score 82 goals for Hibernian, making 145 appearances.

WEDNESDAY 23rd JANUARY 2002

10,000 fans at a freezing Easter Road witnessed an exciting yet ultimately deflating match, as Franck Sauzee's miserable run in the Hibs hot-seat continued against Aberdeen. Aberdeen scored after 17 minutes through Dadi then Hibs equalised just one minute later after a fine effort by Paco Luna. Robbie Winters restored Aberdeen's lead ten minutes later but Derek Townsley equalised for Hibernian just before the break. Guntveit put the 'Dons 3-2 up after 48 mins in this exciting match, then Paco Luna scored Hibs' third equaliser of the night with a header after 68 minutes. The game was headed for what would have been a well-deserved draw for both sides, until Aberdeen were awarded a penalty in injury time. Typical of Hibernian's luck at the time, Nick Colgan saved the penalty only for Darren Mackie to score the rebound, taking the three points back to Aberdeen, Hibs losing the game 4-3.

SATURDAY 24th JANUARY 1948

Hibs manager Willie McCartney collapsed and died in Coatbridge during Hibs' Scottish Cup match against Albion Rovers at Cliftonhill.

Despite his tragic death, Hibs became only the second team outwith the Old Firm since 1904 to win the Scottish League Championship when they lifted the trophy three months later. McCartney's Hibs team was one of the best that Hibs have ever had, and to this day fans speculate about 'what might have been', had he lived longer.

SATURDAY 25th JANUARY 2003

Hibernian made the trip to Tannadice to play Dundee Utd in the third round of the Scottish Cup. Hibs started well, striker Tom McManus running United's defence ragged and midfielder Grant Brebner scoring twice to send Hibs in 2-0 up at half-time and seemingly on their way to the next round. Bobby Williamson's men then contrived to throw away the two-goal lead in the last 20 minutes, a deflected Stephen O'Donnell shot and a Jim Hamilton penalty drawing the Arabs level. The tie looked to be heading for a replay in Edinburgh until three minutes from full time, when Grant Brebner completed his hat-trick by heading the winner, to give the Hibees a 3-2 win.

SATURDAY 26th JANUARY 1985

Winter weather had decimated the weekend's Scottish Cup fixtures, Hibs' trip to Tannadice and Celtic's match against Highland League side Inverness Thistle were among the games called off, but at the time, Hibs were one of a few clubs in Scotland who had undersoil heating. A last-minute friendly bounce-game was organised at Easter Road against Celtic, with 5,000 fans attending despite the fixture's hasty arrangement and limited advertising available in the days of old-media. Hibs thrashed Celtic 6-3, with Ally 'Benny' Brazil scoring a rare hat-trick. Hibs boss John Blackley was in England that day on a scouting mission, so Hibs were managed by his assistant, Tommy Craig.

WEDNESDAY 27th JANUARY 2010

Hibs were still serious title contenders as they travelled to Celtic Park to play Tony Mowbray's Celtic team. At first it looked like déjà-vu in Glasgow, as Celtic took an early lead through Georgios Samaras. John Hughes' Hibs team competed well though, and got an equaliser before half-time through Irishman Anthony Stokes. The game looked set to finish as a draw, until Danny Galbraith sprung Celtic's offside trap in the dying minutes of the match to slip the ball into the Celtic net, sending the Hibs fans into wild delirium, the Hibees heading back to Edinburgh with all three points after a 2-1 win. Hibs finished fourth that season and qualified for Europe, despite a bad dip in form after this victory.

SUNDAY 28th JANUARY 1990

Hibs won their first trophy since 1972, when they won the Tennents Sixes indoor tournament at the SECC in Glasgow, after disposing of Hearts in a dramatic semi-final penalty shoot-out. St Mirren were Hibs' opponents in the final, which finished 2-0. John Collins, Andy Goram and Paul Kane were Hibs' outstanding performers, the latter being the popular tournament's top-scorer, netting eight times, and only being denied a ninth when the hooter that sounded the end of the final went, just before his last-gasp shot crossed the goal-line.

SATURDAY 28th JANUARY 2012

45,000 fans at Ibrox saw James McPake make his Hibernian debut after arriving from Coventry City. Pat Fenlon's men were well beaten, losing the game 4-0 in the end, McPake marking his debut by being red-carded with 20 minutes to go, with Hibs 2-0 down at the time. This was the last time that Hibernian played the old version of Glasgow Rangers, Hibs' bottom six finish meaning that the clubs didn't meet again that season.

SATURDAY 29th JANUARY 2000

Hibs faced Dunfermline Athletic in the third round of the Scottish Cup at Easter Road, cheered on by just over 10,000 fans. Kenny Miller gave Hibs the lead after just two minutes, only for David Graham to equalise for the Fifers on 30 minutes. Grant Brebner restored Hibs' lead just before the interval. The second half saw Easter Road battered by a gale, and also saw Dunfermline completely outclassed. Young Ian Murray, making his home debut for Hibs, scored his first Hibs goal with his first touch of the ball, knocking in a Kenny Miller effort which had been blocked on the line, to make it 3-2 to Hibs, then full-back Derek Collins also got his first goal for Hibernian, with a cool chip in the dying minutes, to send Hibs through to the next round, the tie finishing Hibs 4 Dunfermline 1.

SATURDAY 30th JANUARY 1965

Easter Road was packed with 43,500 fans to see Jock Stein's Hibernian beat Rangers 1-0, with a goal from Neil Martin. Stein's Hibs had already beaten the 'Gers 4-2 at Ibrox earlier in the season and also knocked the Govan side out of the Scottish Cup a few weeks after this 1-0 home league win, in Stein's last match as Hibs boss.

SATURDAY 30th JANUARY 1993

A league encounter saw Hibs and Rangers play out an enthralling match, amid a white-hot atmosphere, despite the freezing weather and strong winds. Rangers had the best of the first half, scoring just one minute before half-time through Mark Hateley. Hibs improved in the second half and equalised through Pat McGinlay after 70 minutes, causing a huge but safe surge on the terracing. Trevor Steven restored Rangers' lead just 30 seconds later, then Hately scored again within 60 seconds, with a header from two yards. Hibs fought back and Darren Jackson scored a volley from a tight angle after a 'stramash' five minutes later. Ally McCoist netted for Rangers with just five minutes left to put them 4-2 up, then Pat McGinlay blasted in Hibs' third in injury time, the match finishing 4-3 to Rangers. Both sets of fans got their money's worth, particularly with six goals in the last 20 minutes, but Hibs were left to rue many missed chances, and some naive goalkeeping from Chris Reid. Nevertheless, Hibs left the field to chants of 'Hibees, Hibees, Hibees' from many fans who had stayed behind to applaud a valiant effort.

SATURDAY 31st JANUARY 1981

A mindnumbingly tedious Division One encounter at Easter Road against Berwick Rangers saw Bertie Auld's Hibees draw 0-0 with 'the wee rangers'. Just 2,000 fans were at the game. Midfielder Iain Hendry made his Hibs debut in this match, and was taken off with a broken leg after just 20 seconds! He only ever made one more appearance for Hibs, as a substitute in a 2-1 win away to Partick Thistle over a year later, before he was sold to Nuneaton Borough.

SATURDAY 31st JANURY 1987

In front of a bumper crowd of 16,500 Hibs disposed of Dunfermline Athletic in the Scottish Cup. The fifers had been on an upturn of late

STEVEN FLETCHER CELEBRATES ANOTHER GOAL FOR HIBS

and provided a stiff challenge for Hibs before the Edinburgh side prevailed with a two goal margin. Mickey Weir and Paul Kane were the Hibs goalscorers.

SATURDAY 31st JANUARY 1998

Battling relegation, Jim Duffy's Hibs side visited Fir Park, and started the match well, going 2-0 up with early strikes by Stevie Crawford and Barry Lavety. Alas, that was a mere distraction to Alex Mcleish's Steelmen. Motherwell routed Hibs 6-2 in the end, the inept Hibees playing like the division one team that they were shortly going to become. One newspaper back page which featured the match ran with the headline 'Next Stop Boghead', in reference to just how bad Hibs were under Duffy. Duffy was sacked at a meeting the very next day, and that was announced to the press that Monday. Billy McNeil took temporary charge of Hibs while a replacement was sought. Ironically, that replacement would turn out to be Alex Mcleish, the very manager whose team had sealed Duffy's fate.

WEDNESDAY 31st JANUARY 2007

Neutral Tynecastle was the venue for this League Cup semi-final between Hibs and St Johnstone, who had already knocked-out Rangers at Ibrox. A near capacity crowd saw Steven Fletcher volley the Hibees into an early lead, but Jason Scotland headed the plucky Saints level 15 minutes from full-time. John Collins made two tactical substitutions midway through the second half when he realised that St Johnstone had changed their shape to combat Hibs, and it was eventually to pay-off, despite Scotland's equaliser. The match went into extra-time and David Murphy scored with a free-kick in the 92nd minute, before Benji scored in the last minute to give Hibs a hard-earned but deserved 3-1 victory and a place in the League Cup Final, where they would face Kilmarnock.

SATURDAY 31st JANUARY 2015

Hibs were at home to Raith Rovers on league business, and appeared to have done enough to secure the points with a goal from transfer window signing Martin Boyle just before half-time. The wide player had arrived in a swap for Alex Harris who had gone in the opposite direction to Dundee. Hibs commanded the match, but a lack of composure in front of goal meant that they were defending a precarious single goal advantage going into the final minutes. It was to prove costly as well. Heading into injury time, the pantomime villan of the peace – Christian Nade, a former Hearts player – equalised for the Fife side.

HIBERNIAN FC
On This Day

FEBRUARY

SATURDAY 1st FEBRUARY 1936

Hibs visited Alexandria to play a relatively new team, Vale Ocoba, in the first round of the Scottish Cup. Whilst the team was relatively new – Ocoba was an acronym for Old Church Old Boys Association – they had links to the former Vale of Leven club, with whom Hibernian had crossed swords in the past. This incarnation was not as threatening and Hibs ran out 3-1 winners with two goals from Paddy Farrell to add to one by Rab Walls. The crowd was 2,622 creating receipts of £86 1/8d – much less to the hosts than the £150 that Hibernian had offered them to play the game at Easter Road.

TUESDAY 2nd FEBRUARY 1999

While running away with the first division title, Hibs faced a Scottish Cup third round replay against Stirling Albion at Forthbank, having drawn the original tie at Easter Road 1-1. Hibs' 'sexy soccer' proved ineffectual for once, and Albion took the lead in the first half through David McCallum. Hibs piled on the pressure and equalised through Russell Latapy, many in the stadium then expected Hibs to go on and win. Hibs gained the ascendancy, but, it was a former Hibee who was to be the hero of this match, Chris Jackson blasting home the winner in the second half to knock Hibs out, 2-1. Hibs' superb league form had left many fans expecting a good cup-run in season 98-99, but it wasn't to be. In the wider scheme of things, the result was a blip, as Hibs stormed their way to the division one title and promotion.

SATURDAY 3rd FEBRUARY 1996

Alex Miller took his team to Glasgow to play Celtic in the league. In purple and green strips, Hibs took the lead on 35 minutes after a great Darren Jackson strike finished off a fine counter attack involving Kevin 'Crunchie' McAllister and Keith Wright. Hibs led 1-0 at the interval but in the second half all 'went to pot' in bizarre circumstances. With Hibs still leading 1-0, a horrible mid-air accidental clash of heads saw John Collins of Celtic and Hibs' 'keeper Jim Leighton have to leave the field for treatment. Scorer Darren Jackson donned the gloves and took over in goal, and was unfortunate to fumble a cross to allow Pierre Van Hooijdonk to equalise for the Hoops on the hour mark. Farce then ensued at a

Celtic throw, as referee Sandy Roy refused to let Jim Leighton onto the pitch after treatment, despite Darren Jackson having taken off the goalie jersey and returned to outfield, assuming that Leighton was coming back on. The referee allowed play to continue despite Hibs having no goalkeeper, both sides looking puzzled. Celtic scored while Hibs were without a 'keeper, but the linesman intervened and the goal was chopped off, despite there being nothing in the game's rules about each team having to have a goalkeeper on. For once, it seemed, Hibs had benefited from a refereeing error in Glasgow. Leighton then returned to the game, and there was no doubt about Celtic's winning goal on 67 minutes, Paul McStay's magnificent volley from 20 yards beating Leighton all ends up, to give the Hoops a narrow 2-1 win over the battling Hibees.

SUNDAY 3rd FEBRUARY 2013

Irish midfielder Gary Deegan's 30-yard strike just after half-time was enough to give Pat Fenlon's men a 1-0 victory over Aberdeen, in their Scottish Cup fifth round match at Easter Road. Deegan had only recently returned to first-team action after suffering a broken jaw after an unprovoked sectarian assault on him in Edinburgh city-centre in late 2012.

SATURDAY 4th FEBRUARY 2006

The Scottish Cup saw Rangers host Hibernian in the fourth round. A large Hibs support travelled to Ibrox this time, thanks mainly to the fact that Hibs had won their last two matches against the Govan side, with league wins already that season at Ibrox in August and at Easter Road in November. Hibs also had more fans present because the Scottish Cup allows a bigger allocation of away support tickets (20%) than league or League Cup games. Tony Mowbray's side used the same tactics as on their previous visit to Govan, frustrating Rangers in the first half to go in 0-0 at half-time. Rangers missed many chances in the first half, and were punished four minutes after the re-start, Garry O'Connor giving Hibs the lead. Ivan Sproule scored his fourth goal at Ibrox of the season to put Hibs 2-0 up after an hour, and New Zealand striker Chris Killen completed the rout with Hibs' third goal 12 minutes from time. Once again, Mowbray's men had 'suckered' Rangers tactically. Hibernian won the tie 3-0 and progressed to the quarter-finals. The Hibbies in the Broomloan stand spent much of the second half teasing the home support by lampooning their own songs and chants.

SATURDAY 5th FEBRUARY 1994

Hibs humbled the once-mighty Aberdeen 3-1 at Easter Road, in front of just under 10,000 fans. An inspired performance by midfielder Danny Lennon in a rare start, who also scored, and a brace from Keith Wright, had Hibs on easy-street. Duncan Shearer netted The Dons' consolation with a fine effort in the second half.

THURSDAY 5th FEBRUARY 2004

Injury ravaged Hibs, having already beaten Celtic at Easter Road in the quarter finals of the League Cup, conquered the other half of the old firm by beating Rangers on penalties in the semi-final at Hampden, live on Channel 5. Michael Mols had given the Ibrox side the lead at half-time, but Hibs equalised through Stephen Dobbie in the second half, and had the rub of the green in extra-time and in the shoot-out to go through to the final against Livingston. Hibs' 'keeper Daniel Anderson was the hero, saving a Mikel Arteta penalty in the first half before once again turning on the style to keep out the champions in the nail-biting penalty competition, cheered on by 7,000 diehard Hibs fans, who were outnumbered 3-1 by the Rangers fans.

SUNDAY 6th FEBRUARY 1977

Partick Thistle visited Easter Road in the Scottish Cup third round, played on a Sunday for the first time. 13,700 supporters saw Eddie Turnbull's team comprehensively defeat the 'Jags 3-0, with goals from Des Bremner, Ally MacLeod and Bobby Smith.

WEDNESDAY 6th FEBRUARY 2002

Under new boss Franck Sauzee, the Hibees travelled to Hampden to take on Ayr United in the League Cup semi-final. Fewer than 12,000 fans were at the game, and the ghostly atmosphere was matched only by both sides' dreadful football. Fans' misery was compounded as the match finished 0-0 and went into extra-time, with Ayr scoring the only goal of the game in its first half, from the penalty spot.

The game had been played at Hampden on the insistence of Alex Mcleish, who had then departed for Rangers. A miserable night for Hibs, with many fans left wondering 'what might've been' had Sauzee's team triumphed and reached the final.

SATURDAY 7th FEBRUARY 1920

Hibs visited Armadale on Scottish Cup business, and were on the receiving end of a giant-killing shock from their West Lothian opponents. A strong Hibs side including much of the team who would make successive cup finals in 1923 and 1924 played, and in truth Hibs dominated their lower league opponents, and were unfortunate not to score on several occasions, whilst Armadale scored on a rare foray into the visitors' half. Davy Gordon, the Hibs manager who had taken over upon the death of Dan McMichael in 1919, was to move on at the end of the following season.

SATURDAY 8th FEBRUARY 1919

Hibs played hosts to Dumbarton, and recorded a rare victory in an otherwise forgettable season. As soldiers from the continent began returning home, the green jerseys recorded only five wins in their 38 game league programme, finishing rock-bottom of the 18 team set-up. Future manager Bobby Templeton played full-back in this team, whilst the delightfully named Horace Williams scored the only goal of the game.

SATURDAY 9th FEBRUARY 1935

Hibs were on Scottish Cup duty on this day, in a second round tie at Easter Road against opponents from Inverness – Clachnacuddin, who remain the oldest senior football team in the city since the merger of Caledonian and Thistle. The gulf in ability between the sides showed, and Hibs recorded their favourite 7-0 scoreline. Hibs' goalscorers were Rab Walls with a brace, singles from William Black and John Smith and a hat-trick from Alfie Anderson.

SATURDAY 10th FEBRUARY 1951

As hard as it might be to believe now, Hibs once won a Scottish Cup tie at Ibrox in front of – wait for it – 102,342 spectators - a record that is unlikely ever to be beaten. This second round tie showed the skills of the Famous Five at their imperious best and goals from Gordon Smith, Bobby Johnstone and Eddie Turnbull sealed an easy 3-2 victory for the Edinburgh side.

SATURDAY 11th FEBRUARY 1961

The second round of the Scottish Cup saw East of Scotland League side Peebles Rovers visit Easter Road to take on Hugh Shaw's Hibs team. People talk of the romance of the cup, but in this match, there was only slaughter. Joe Baker scored nine goals, John Baxter and Willie Ormond bagged a brace apiece and there were single goals by Sammy Baird and Johnny McLeod as the Hibees won 15-1! This match is Hibernian's record victory in a competitive match, but it's not Peebles Rovers' record defeat – that had come the season before when they were mauled 23-2 by Partick Thistle at Firhill.

SATURDAY 12th FEBRUARY 1944

Hibs fought out a hard earned draw at Parkhead in the Scottish Southern League. In a poor game, Willie McCartney's team had allowed the Hoops to establish a two goal lead with 15 minutes to go and the result looked certain. However, this Hibs side was made of stronger stuff and goals from Jimmy Caskie and Hugh Colvan in the last twelve minutes of the match secured a 2-2 draw.

SATURDAY 13th FEBRUARY 1971

Dave Ewing's Hibees were in fourth round Scottish Cup action against Hearts at Tynecastle, in front of just over 30,000 fans. John Hazel's diving header gave Hibs the lead but Hearts equalised through a header of their own from Hegarty. Arthur Duncan's stunning left-foot strike gave Hibs a 2-1 cup victory over their city rivals.

SATURDAY 14th FEBRUARY 1987

Goals from Eddie May, Steve Cowan, Joe McBride and Mickey Weir helped Alex Miller's men beat struggling Clydebank 4-1 at Easter Road in the league. Barely 5,000 fans were there to see this walkover by Alex Miller's men. The Bankies have long since dropped out of senior football, but still exist as a 'newco' in the lower-leagues.

FRIDAY 15th FEBRUARY 1985

In a friendly match at Easter Road, John Blackley's men beat Soviet side Dynamo Moscow 2-0, thanks to a double from striker Gordon Durie.

SATURDAY 16th FEBRUARY 2002

Franck Sauzee managed Hibernian for what would be the last time, as Hibs drew 1-1 with Dunfermline Athletic at Easter Road in the league, in front of just under 10,000 fans. Hampshire had given the 'Pars the lead after 60 mins, but Derek Townsley equalised for Hibs with ten minutes remaining. It wasn't enough to save Sauzee. A legend as a player, his managerial spell at Hibs lasted only 69 days, during which Hibernian only won one game, a Scottish Cup replay against Stranraer. His record as manager was played 15, won once, drawn six and lost eight.

SATURDAY 17th FEBRUARY 1940

In this first season of wartime football, Hibs secured a narrow victory over Kings Park, who were a senior team from Stirling who unfortunately did not survive the war. Their Forthbank ground was damaged by a 2,000lb Hermann bomb dropped from a Luftwaffe plane in 1941. Hibs won this game 2-1, with a penalty inside the first minute from Rab Walls added to by a late goal for Charles Birse. Walls missed a second-half penalty for Hibs.

SATURDAY 18th FEBRUARY 1967

Round two of the Scottish Cup saw nearly 30,000 fans at Easter Road as Bob Shankly's Hibees took on Berwick Rangers. Many expected an upset, as 'the wee rangers' had knocked out Glasgow Rangers in the previous round, in what is still one of the biggest episodes of giant-killing in the history of Scottish football. A Jimmy Scott goal just before half-time was enough to give Hibs a 1-0 victory in this match, Scott also missing a penalty in the later stages of the game.

SATURDAY 19th FEBRUARY 1972

An interesting league match unfolded at Brockville between Falkirk and Hibernian. A Falkirk defender named Alex Ferguson broke Alex Cropley's ankle in this match, Cropley missing the rest of the season. Hibs took the lead through Johnny Hamilton after just ten seconds! The Bairns fought back with goals from Alex Ferguson and Doug Somner but it wasn't enough to stop Turnbull's Tornadoes winning the game 3-2, with goals from Alan Gordon and a late diving-header from Joe Baker. Falkirk's Ferguson was sent-off for arguing with the referee after Baker's winner. You probably now know that Falkirk defender as Sir Alex Ferguson, one of Scotland's greatest ever football managers.

SUNDAY 20th FEBRUARY 1994

Easter Road was the venue for an all-Edinburgh Scottish Cup Fourth Round tie between Hibs and Hearts, shown live on TV throughout the UK. Hibs, who had been struggling in this fixture and had looked jaded since losing the Cup Final to Rangers the previous October, were looking to end a win-less run against Hearts that had lasted since early 1989. John Robertson gave Hearts an early lead, then Keith Wright equalised for Hibs just before the interval. Hearts' backs were against the wall for most of the second half, then, with only four minutes to go and with the match heading for a midweek replay at Tynecastle, a dreadful error in judgement by Hibs defender Dave Beaumont allowed Hearts substitute Wayne Foster an unimpeded run at goal from which he scored, much to the jubilation of the away fans. Foster had hitherto been a figure of ridicule to fans of both clubs, but this goal sealed his place in Edinburgh football folklore.

SUNDAY 21st FEBRUARY 1988

A rare live BBC televised game saw Hibs travel to Celtic Park to take on the Hoops in the Scottish Cup fourth round. Hibs wore green shorts instead of white shorts with their traditional 'home' kit in this game, which had a crowd of just over 30,000. The match was largely uneventful and degenerated into a midfield slog, and finished 0-0. Celtic won the replay at Easter Road 1-0, Billy Stark heading the decisive goal late in the game.

TUESDAY 21st FEBRUARY 1995

Scotland's fringe players got their chance in a B international against Northern Ireland played at Easter Road. A freezing but boisterous 'home' support saw Scotland thump the Irishmen 3-0 with goals from Stephen Wright and a goal apiece from Hibs players Darren Jackson and Steven Tweed. The latter two's goals triggering an impromptu chorus of 'Hibees' from the East Terrace, despite the match being an international.

WEDNESDAY 22nd FEBRUARY 1961

The mighty Barcelona visited Easter Road for a UEFA Cup (Fairs Cup) quarter-final second leg tie, the first leg at The Nou Camp having finished an astonishing 4-4! Easter Road was packed with 45,000 fans for what was a memorable match, Hibs winning 3-2 on the night to go through to the semi-finals 7-6 on aggregate. Hibs' goals came from Joe Baker, Tommy Preston and a penalty by Bobby Kinloch. Barcelona's scorers were Martinez and Kocsis. Hibs would play Italian giants AS Roma in the semi-finals.

SATURDAY 23rd FEBRUARY 1980

Peter Cormack made his second Hibs 'debut', ten years after leaving the club, as the Hibees took on Dundee Utd in the league at Tannadice in front of just under 8,000 fans. It wasn't a happy return for Cormack, who had re-joined the club on a two-year deal as player-coach. Dundee Utd won the match 1-0 thanks to a Willie Pettigrew strike just before half-time. Hibs' 'keeper Jim McArthur was the 'man of the match'.

SATURDAY 23rd FEBRUARY 1991

Hibernian were in Perth to play St Johnstone in the Scottish Cup fourth round. St Johnstone won the match 2-1, with Roddy Grant scoring the winner in the 90th minute. Brian Hamilton was Hibs' scorer. This was striker Keith Houchen's last game for Hibs, as he was sent-off for an assault on St Johnstone's Tommy Turner and then reacted angrily to the Hibs fans on his way off the pitch. He had been on his last warning at Hibs since a similar incident away to Raith Rovers in the League Cup. Neil Cooper was also red-carded in this Scottish Cup tie.

SATURDAY 24th FEBRUARY 1906

Hibs and Partick Thistle met for the third time, in the second round of the Scottish Cup in an attempt to settle the tie, this time at neutral Ibrox. The crowd was reported as disappointing, and the receipts were only £232! Both teams were unchanged from the previous two games, and although the 'Jags opened the scoring, they failed to capitalise and missed with two penalty kicks they were awarded. Hibs didn't let them off the hook, and sealed their place in the next round with goals from John Macconachie – from a penalty obviously – and Billy McNeil.

SATURDAY 25th FEBRUARY 2006

Having dumped Rangers out of the Scottish Cup in the previous round, Tony Mowbray's men travelled to Falkirk in the quarter-finals. Hibs took the lead through Derek Riordan after nine minutes and Garry O'Connor doubled the lead after 67 mins. Breen pulled one back for the Bairns three minutes later but the Cabbage demolished their opponents in the last 15 minutes, with goals from Ivan Sproule, Gary Caldwell and substitute Steven Fletcher giving Hibernian a 5-1 victory, setting up a semi-final clash with big-spending city-rivals Hearts.

SATURDAY 26th FEBRUARY 1910

Hibs triumphed in a Scottish Cup tie at Tynecastle, with the only goal of the game being scored by Jim Peggie, early in the second half. The Hibernians – as they were often referred to in the newspapers of the day – had the better of the play throughout the game, and were worthy winners. Hearts did exert some pressure after the Hibs goal, but this soon passed, and Hibs monopolised the play and never looked threatened.

SATURDAY 27th FEBRUARY 1993

Alex Miller's men played Airdrieonians in the league at Easter Road. The Diamonds, managed by former Hearts boss Alex MacDonald and with a team containing several ex-Hearts players, were beginning to become something of a bogey-team for Hibs, having denied Hibs a possible domestic cup-double the previous season by winning the quarter-final between the sides 2-0 at Easter Road. On this occasion, though, Hibernian thumped the Lanarkshire side, whose notorious physical style of play was more akin to GAA than soccer, 3-1, with Hibs' goals coming from a Pat McGinlay penalty and a double from Darren Jackson.

SATURDAY 27th FEBRUARY 2010

An SPL draw between Hibs and St Johnstone saw the last game at Easter Road for the old East Stand, still commonly referred to as 'the terracing', even though it had been seated in 1994 to comply with The Taylor Report. The traditional home of the more vocal element of the Hibs support was to be demolished to make way for a new stand which would take stadium capacity up to over 20,000. The 1-1 draw, with Anthony Stokes scoring for John Hughes' Hibs, saw emotional scenes at the final whistle, as the fans on the 'terracing' sang 'East Stand 'til I die', many fans taking their seats home as souvenirs. Hibs home-form nosedived for a couple of seasons after this stand, feared by opposition players over the years, closed and was replaced, but by 2014, the atmosphere was back.

SATURDAY 28th FEBRUARY 1953

'A COMBE-OUT AT AIRDRIE' proclaimed the *Glasgow Evening Times*, as Hibs ran riot with a 7-3 victory at Broomfield to maintain their position at the top of the league by two points from second placed East Fife. Bobby Combe, the sixth member of the Famous Five, deputised for the injured Lawrie Reilly and stamped his authority on the game with four of the Hibs goals. The other goalscorers were Gordon Smith, and Bobby Johnstone with a double.

SATURDAY 28th FEBRUARY 2015

Hibs continued their fine unbeaten going, with a well deserved victory at Station Park on a rare league excursion to Alloa. Scott Allan scored the only game of the game in the 26th minute in front of a crowd just over two thousand.

SATURDAY 29th FEBRUARY 1908

On this leap day, Hibs entertained Port Glasgow Athletic, a short lived senior team from the west coast town. Hibs won 2-1 with both goals scored by Paddy Hagan, one from the penalty spot. Hibs were without goalkeeper Harry Rennie and full-back Jimmy Main, who were on international duty with the Scottish League side against England at Birmingham. Scotland lost that match 2-0.

WEDNESDAY 29th FEBRUARY 2000

Hibs easily seen off Clydebank in a Scottish Cup replay at Cappielowe, where Clydebank were playing their fixtures. The nomadic west coast club had been forced to play their manager in goals after being refused permission by the SFA to sign an emergency goalkeeper. It was surprising that the struggling part-timers had managed to take Hibs to a replay, but John Rowbotham, a referee who was notorious for some strange decisions had taken it upon himself to send off Tom Smith in the first leg for an innoccous tackle. Goals on the night from Franck Sauzee, Stuart Lovell and Dirk Diggler Lehmann gave Hibs a convincing 3-0 victory.

HIBERNIAN FC
On This Day

MARCH

SATURDAY 1st MARCH 1958

It might not have been the biggest win that Hibs ever secured at the home of their local rivals, but their victory in this Scottish Cup tie was just as remarkable. A bumper crowd of over 41,000 turned up for this third round game, and most expected Hearts to win comfortably given that they were well on their way to the league title. Football has a funny way of not going to the script and it was to be so on this occasion, as 17-year-old Joe Baker – in his first season in the first team – produced a quite stunning performance to score all the Greens' goals in a 4-3 victory. Only Eddie Turnbull and Willie Ormond of the Famous Five remained, as Lawrie Reilly neared the end of his injury shortened career and missed out. Gordon Marshall senior, father of the Hibs goalkeeping coach of the same name, was in goals for Hearts.

SATURDAY 2nd MARCH 1991

Struggling Hibs faced struggling St Mirren at Easter Road in front of a 4,000-strong crowd. Injury-ravaged Hibs fielded a very much 'make do and mend' type team for this supposed relegation 'four-pointer'. Paul Wright gave the Hibees an early lead from the penalty-spot. However, a fightback by the Buddies saw the Paisley side race into a 3-1 lead by the 60th minute, with goals from Kinnaird, Martin and Torfason. Many stunned Hibbies headed for the exits when Saints' third goal went in but that exodus halted when Gordon Hunter pulled one back for Hibs with a superb 16-yard volley on 66 mins. Paul Wright equalised for the Cabbage seven minutes from full-time, to earn what looked like a deserved draw, but then substitute Gareth Evans rifled home a winning goal deep in injury-time to give all two points to Hibernian. (Two points were awarded for a win back in those days, not three). Hibs had won the 'relegation battle' with a marvellous fightback, but ultimately, there was no relegation that season, as the top flight was extended to 12 teams. In any case, it wasn't league reconstruction which saved Hibs from the theoretical drop – they finished six points above bottom club St Mirren anyway.

SUNDAY 3rd MARCH 2013

BBC Scotland televised this live Scottish Cup quarter-final clash between Hibs and Kilmarnock at Rugby Park, with Pat Fenlon's men looking to reach their second consecutive final. Despite awful defending by the home side, this match is best remembered for Leigh Griffiths' hat-trick. Griffiths gave Hibs the lead after 15 minutes only for Dayton to equalise ten minutes later. Matt Done restored Hibs' lead just before half-time, only for Killie to level the match at 2-2 with 17 minutes remaining, via a Paul Heffernan penalty. Griffiths grabbed his second goal of the game with eight minutes to go, then Kilmarnock's Barbour was red-carded for a foul on the striker. A few minutes later, Griffiths completed his hat-trick with a last minute penalty to give Hibs a 4-2 win. The huge, noisy Hibs support who had made the trip to Ayrshire were in fine voice throughout, and made the trip back east after the game having seen Fenlon's Hibs ultimately steamroller Kilmarnock. Another visit to Hampden beckoned for the Hibees.

SATURDAY 4th MARCH 1933

Hibs had all but secured promotion and the second division title, while Hearts were flying high when the two sides met at Easter Road in this eagerly anticipated fourth round Scottish Cup tie. An impressive near ground record attendance of just under 34,000 saw the sides play out a goalless draw. Hibs had been relegated for the first time in 1931, and most had expected that Hibs would bounce straight back up, but their first season in the lower league had proved far more trickier than expected. This season had seen much improvement and Hibs could count themselves unlucky not to triumph in this tie, losing the replay 0-2.

SATURDAY 5th MARCH 1960

Hibs travelled to Firs Park in Falkirk (not to be confused with Motherwell's Fir Park) for a Scottish Cup third round tie against second division East Stirlingshire, who were just beginning to re-establish themselves as a senior club following decades of turmoil. The Shire were no match for Hugh Shaw's men, who won the match 3-0, goals coming from Des Fox and a double from Joe Baker. Over 8,000 fans packed the tiny ground for the tie.

SUNDAY 5th MARCH 2000

Celtic had just sacked one half of their managerial 'dream team' of John Barnes and Kenny Dalglish, leaving Dalglish in charge for the remainder of the season. Easter Road was the venue for this evening kick-off in the league. Alex Mcleish's side led 1-0 at half-time through a Pat McGinlay strike, and young Kenny Miller doubled the Hibees' advantage on the hour. Australian striker Mark Viduka scored demoralised Celtic's late consolation and the match finished 2-1 to Hibs. Hibs fans on the East Stand spent most of the game singing the simple ditty 'you're no very good' to the visiting support.

SATURDAY 6th MARCH 1965

Jock Stein's Hibernian side faced Rangers at Easter Road in front of just over 47,000 fans in the quarter-finals of the Scottish Cup. Hibs won the match 2-1 with goals from John Baxter and Willie Hamilton. This was Jock Stein's last game in charge of Hibs before he left for Celtic. Stein's is a great 'what if' when it comes to Hibernian, he was only at the helm for a short time, but worked miracles, and bagged Hibs the Summer Cup, a big trophy at the time. He won 62% of his games as Hibs boss, making him, statistically, the best manager in Hibernian's history. His record was played 50, won 31, drew 8, lost 11, Hibs scoring 118 goals and conceding 68 in that time. He went on to become the greatest Scottish manager of all-time.

SATURDAY 6th MARCH 1982

2,500 fans at Firhill saw Bertie Auld's Hibernian beat Partick Thistle 2-1, Gordon Rae and Craig Paterson netting to give the Hibees all two points. Iain Hendry made his second and final appearance for Hibs, coming on as a substitute, over a year after breaking his leg.

WEDNESDAY 7th MARCH 1973

Another great European night at Easter Road saw Hibs play Yugoslavia's Hadjuk Split in the Cup Winners Cup quarter-final first leg at Easter Road, cheered on by nearly 30,000 fans. Eddie Turnbull's men won the pulsating match 4-2, goals coming from Arthur Duncan and an Alan Gordon hat-trick. It looked like Hibs just might go all the way in the competition, just a year after Rangers had won it. Alas, it all went wrong in the second leg in Yugoslavia, Hibs losing 3-0 and going out 5-4 on aggregate. John Blackley scored an own goal and several Hibs players froze on the night, including goalie Jim Herriot, who never played for Hibs again. Nevertheless, the run was a great achievement as the Cup Winners Cup was a prestigious trophy back then. Hadjuk Split lost to Leeds in the semi-final.

SATURDAY 7th MARCH 1992

The quarter- final of the Scottish Cup saw Airdrieonians visit Easter Road, with Hibs looking to 'do the double' by winning the Scottish Cup, having won the League Cup the previous October. It wasn't to be. Tommy McIntyre had a penalty saved by Airdrie 'keeper John Martin, and two counter attacks saw the Diamonds score, to win the tie 2-0.

SATURDAY 8th MARCH 1986

Holders Celtic visited Easter Road to take on the Hibees in this Scottish Cup quarter-final, watched by 20,000 fans. Celtic went in 1-0 up at the interval thanks to a Brian McClair strike. The second half saw six goals and two penalties, with three of the goals coming in the last six minutes. The atmosphere in the ground was described simply as 'electric'. Steve Cowan equalised for Hibs after 51 minutes, Hibs going 'down the slope' in the second half. Mark McGhee put Celtic back in front nine minutes later. Gordon Chisholm headed Hibs level at 2-2 after 70 minutes and then Steve Cowan scored again, with a penalty in the 84th minute. Celtic got a penalty themselves just 120 seconds later, which McClair duly scored, and the tie looked headed for a replay until substitute Eddie May headed in Colin Harris' cross in the last minute, to give Hibs a 4-3 win. Hibs would play Aberdeen in the semi-final.

SATURDAY 9th MARCH 1974

Scottish Cup quarter-final action at Easter Road saw a thrilling match between Hibernian and Dundee. 29,000 fans witnessed an Alan Gordon hat-trick, amid what ended as a thrilling 3-3 draw and fantastic cup tie. Hibernian only ever lost twice in games where Alan Gordon scored. Unfortunately, Eddie Turnbull's men lost the replay at Dens Park, 0-3.

SATURDAY 10th MARCH 1979

There were 22,600 fans at Easter toad to see Hibs knock Hearts out of the Scottish Cup at the quarter-final stage. A George Stewart header and a superb strike in the second half from Gordon Rae won this cup-derby for the Hibees, who went on to reach the final. Derek O'Connor scored Hearts' consolation goal late on.

SATURDAY 10th MARCH 2001

Alex Mcleish's team headed to Rugby Park to face Kilmarnock in this Scottish Cup quarter-final tie. Hibs were enjoying a great season, but found Killie difficult to break down and dangerous on the counter-attack. The match was at stalemate and heading for a replay at Easter Road, until substitute Tom McManus headed in an injury-time winner for the Cabbage, much to the delight of the big away support. McManus had thus far scored in every round of the tournament. After the match, Killie boss Bobby Williamson was gracious in his interview, saying simply 'I hope Hibs win it'.

SATURDAY 11th MARCH 1995

Just 3,500 fans at tiny Ochilview saw Stenhousemuir host Hibs in the Scottish Cup quarter-finals. Many Hibs fans watched the game via a live 'beamback' at Murrayfield Ice Rink. The Warriors had already shocked Scotland by beating Aberdeen 2-0 at their tiny stadium in the previous round and many in the media were predicting that Hibernian would suffer the same fate. They didn't. Hibs won the match easily, goals from Kevin Harper (2), Joe Tortolano and Michael O'Neill giving Alex Miller's men a 4-0 win and sending them into the semi-finals.

SATURDAY 12th MARCH 1927

In a tousy affair at Easter Road, Hibs triumphed over the recently renamed Dundee United (they had originally been formed as Dundee Hibs in homage to the Edinburgh team). Hibs made heavy weather of their struggling opponents who were flirting with relegation near the bottom of the league. Dundee United, who played in white at this time, had twice taken the lead only to be pegged back by goals from Harry Ritchie and Johnny Halligan. Future Wembley Wizard Jimmy Dunn scored the Hibs winner in the closing minutes.

SATURDAY 13th MARCH 2010

Hibernian welcomed Ross County to Easter Road in the quarter-finals of the Scottish Cup. Hibs were without their '12th man', the East Stand, as it had been demolished, hence the crowd of only 9,800. Hibs took an early lead through a Colin Nish header, then Ian Murray scored after 16 minutes – unfortunately, it was an own-goal. Derek Riordan restored Hibs' one-goal lead three minutes later, but the first division Staggies, who had brought 1,600 fans to Edinburgh, more than held their own, and bagged a deserved equaliser through Gardyne ten-minutes from full time. John Hughes' Hibs lost the replay 2-1 up in Dingwall, Ross County scoring the winner in injury time, as the Staggies again clawed back a Hibs lead, Anthony Stokes having put Hibs one-up after 46 minutes. Ross County then knocked out Celtic in the semi-final, before losing the final 3-0 to Dundee Utd.

SUNDAY 14th MARCH 2004

Having already disposed of Celtic and Rangers in the quarter-finals and semi-finals respectively, Hibs faced Livingston at Hampden in the final of the League Cup. Around 40,000 Hibbies were in attendance to witness Bobby Williamson's young Hibs side freeze, losing to Livi 0-2, The Lions' goals coming from Derek Lilley and Jamie McAllister.

SATURDAY 15th MARCH 1919

A struggling Hibs team secured a rare success in this Victory Cup tie against Ayr United. There were just four minutes of this second round tie to be played when Kirkpatrick scored what was to prove the winning goal. This was harsh on the Ayr side who had enjoyed the better of exchanges throughout the game. With the Great War ending just after the start of the 1918/1919 season, it was felt too late to restart the Scottish Cup, so the SFA organised the Victory Cup instead. Hibs weren't to enjoy any better fortune in this tournament – they lost 3-1 to St Mirren in the semi final who went on to beat Hearts in the Final.

SATURDAY 16th MARCH 1985

Davie Hay's title-chasing Celtic side were shocked at home in front of just over 15,000 fans, as John Blackley's Hibernian defeated them 1-0 thanks to a first half strike by Paul Kane. Celtic were truly woeful, but that took nothing away from Hibs' performance. Two Scottish papers described Hibs midfielder Brian Rice as 'world class' in reports after this game. Rice, later in his career, was voted Nottingham Forest's 'worst ever player' in a fans' poll. It's a funny old game.

SATURDAY 17th MARCH 1962

A St Patrick's day clash in the league at Easter Road between Hibs and St Johnstone produced a cracking match, a five-goal thriller which Walter Galbraith's Hibees came out on top in, winning 3-2. Hibs goals were scored by Gerry Baker, John Fraser and Duncan Falconer, in front of about 4,000 fans.

SATURDAY 17th MARCH 2001

High flying Hibs were undone at East End Park in a fascinating clash of styles as the season moved towards the business end of the season. Hibs were forced into a couple of changes as injuries started to take their toll, and Mark Dempsie – the highly rated young centre-back made a rare appearance, as did Lyndon Andrews the compatriot of Russell Latapy from Trinidad who had been so outstanding in the 6-2 defeat of Hearts earlier in the season. Hibs missed the lynch pin of Franck Sauzee, though, and despite a goal from Ian Murray were to go down to a 2-1 defeat.

SATURDAY 18th MARCH 2000

Hearts travelled to Easter Road on the back of a six-game unbeaten run. Former Hibs hero Darren Jackson gave the Jambos the lead with a stunning strike after 25 minutes, but Hibs equalised before half-time through Russell Latapy. Second half goals from Franck Sauzee and Mixu Paatelainen gave the Hibees a 3-1 win in the end. This match is best remembered as the 'Sauzee's Teeth' game, as the big Frenchman lost his front teeth in the process of scoring Hibs second goal.

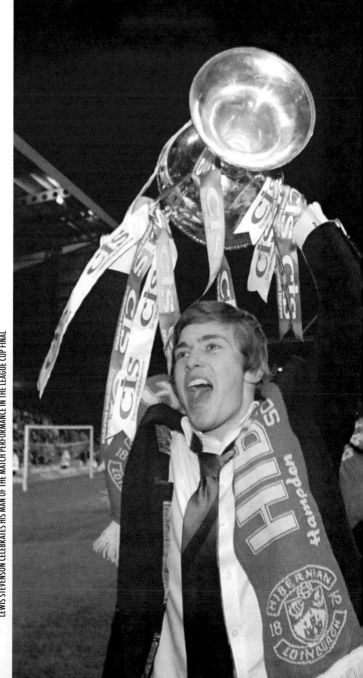

SUNDAY 18th MARCH 2007

John Collins' Hibs side thrashed Jim Jefferies' Kilmarnock 5-1 in a breathtaking display in front of a full-house at Hampden to win the League Cup, the Easter Road side's first major trophy since 1991. Hibs' goals came from Steven Fletcher (2), Benji (2) and skipper Rob Jones. Gordon Greer got Kilmarnock's futile consolation. A moving spectacle after the match saw over 30,000 jubilant Hibs fans sing along to 'Sunshine on Leith' beneath the grey Hampden sky.

SATURDAY 19th MARCH 1949

A star studded Hibs team fell just short in this league game, losing out to Dundee 4-3 at Dens Park. They had started brightly taking an early lead through Eddie Turnbull, and despite being pegged back held a half-time advantage through a goal from Jock Cuthbertson. Hibs had been dominant, and the title challengers looked good for the two points. However a very good Dundee side came back to score three times in six second-half minutes before Eddie Turnbull scored a last minute consolation goal. Dundee finished the season second just a point behind champions Rangers whilst Hibs finished third, ahead of East Fife in fourth.

SATURDAY 20th MARCH 1920

Hibs and Clydebank fought out an entertaining draw in this Scottish League game at Clydeholm Park. Hibs had been reduced to ten men in the first half with the injury to Tommy Kilpatrick, who had been the victim of some over robust tackling. Hibs 'turned' at the half-time break 3-1 down and with the odds stacked against them. Not for the first time, adversity brought out the best in the green jerseys and they recovered with two second-half goals to earn a point. Hugh Shaw, who was to manage the title winning teams of the Fifties, reduced the deficit before Harry Ritchie belted the equalising goal.

SATURDAY 21st MARCH 1998

New manager Alex McLeish faced his old club Motherwell at Easter Road, gaining his first victory as manager. Ironically, he had been brought to Hibs to try to save the club from relegation, Jim Duffy having been sacked after a 6-2 defeat by McLeish's Motherwell. Though this was by no means a classic match, the Hibees winning 1-0 thanks to a Barry Lavety strike despite having David Elliot sent-off, there were signs since Big Eck's arrival that the team had regained its confidence, bolstered by a couple of shrewd loan signings, Man Utd youngster Grant Brebner and experienced former Scotland 'keeper Bryan Gunn. McLeish had also tried to get Mixu Paatelainen from Wolves, but had to wait until September to sign the big Finn.

MONDAY 22nd MARCH 1965

Hearts were top of the table and Hibs were second. Hibs travelled to Celtic Park to play against recently departed manager Jock Stein's side, who had left Easter Road for Glasgow two weeks earlier. Hibernian, now under Bob Shankly, were 4-0 up at half-time thanks to a hat-trick from Neil Martin and an own-goal from Young of Celtic. Bobby Lennox grabbed two consolation goals for Celtic in the second half and it finished Celtic 2 Hibs 4. Hibs had 'proved a point' to their former manager.

WEDNESDAY 23rd MARCH 1977

13,700 fans at Easter Road saw Hibs win the Edinburgh derby 3-1, in a league match which Hearts really needed to win to aid their quest to avoid relegation. Hibs goals came from Ally MacLeod, Bobby Smith and Ally Scott, Hearts' consolation goal coming from Gibson.

SATURDAY 24th MARCH 1990

Alex Miller's men made the trip along the M8 to play Rangers at Ibrox in a Premier League game. Hibs' 'keeper Andy Goram played superbly as Rangers dominated the match, but Hibs' new strike partnership of Paul Wright, recently signed from QPR, and Keith Houchen, always looked dangerous. Against all odds, Hibs won the match 1-0 thanks to a Keith Houchen goal. Houchen is most famous for scoring Coventry City's winning goal in their 3-2 FA Cup Final win over Spurs in 1987, with a spectacular diving header. Alas, Hibbies would see little of what Wright and Houchen could do together, as Wright was injured in the following week's Edinburgh Derby by a disgusting tackle from Hearts' Neil Berry. Wright was out injured for some time and was eventually sold to St Johnstone, while Houchen left Easter Road under a cloud the following season.

SATURDAY 25th MARCH 1939

If you thought that Hibs' poor luck in Scottish Cup semi-finals is a recent trend, you should think again, as this day in history shows. Just months prior to the start of the Second World War, 'McCartney's Babes' took on Clyde at Tynecastle in front of a bumper 39,812 crowd. Hibs had the better chances on the day but a combination of excellent goalkeeping from Jock Brown – later to play for Hibernian, and father to Scottish Rugby internationals Peter and Gordon – and poor luck saw the Glasgow side win 1-0 to go through to the Cup Final – which they duly won in some style against Motherwell.

SATURDAY 26th MARCH 1960

Dundee, managed by future Hibs boss Bob Shankly, thrashed Hugh Shaw's Hibernian team 6-3 at Dens Park in a league match in front of 8,000 fans. In an afternoon to forget for the Hibees, John Baxter was sent-off and goalkeeper Willie Muirhead had an absolute nightmare. Hibs' three goals came from Bobby Johnstone, John Fraser and Joe Baker.

SATURDAY 27th MARCH 1965

Tynecastle was the neutral venue as Bob Shankly's Hibs took on Dunfermline Athletic in the Scottish Cup semi-final, in front of just under 34,000 fans. The Pars won the game 2-0, with goals from Melrose and Smith. The Hibees had a goal ruled-out just after Dunfermline's second goal.

WEDNESDAY 28th MARCH 1979

Just over 16,000 fans were at Tynecastle to see what was actually supposed to have been the Edinburgh New Year derby, which had been postponed because of bad weather. This somewhat belated 'festive' fixture saw Ally MacLeod give the Cabbage the lead after just six minutes. Willie Gibson equalised for Hearts ten minutes later. Ralph Callachan scored what turned out to be the winner for Hibs just before the break, with a speculative cross-come-shot. It finished 2-1 to Hibs. It would be almost a decade before Hibernian beat Hearts at Tynecastle again.

SATURDAY 29th MARCH 1947

In recent times, 'golden goals' were used in major international tournaments to settle tied games, but this was not altogether a recent development and as long ago as 1947 the SFA used a 'next goal the winner' system to settle cup-ties. This meant that when Hibs played Motherwell in the Scottish Cup semi-final the match lasted a whopping 142 minutes, before a freak goal from Hugh Howie settled matters. Eddie Turnbull had given Hibs the lead against the run of play, before Willie Kilmarnock had equalised for the 'Well. Full-back Hugh Howie scored the decisive goal by volleying a clearance from the 'Well goalkeeper straight back over his head from 40 yards out.

SATURDAY 30th MARCH 1940

Hibs triumphed in this wartime local derby with rivals St Bernards in the newly established Scottish Regional League (Eastern Division). Hibs were far too strong for their visitors and were three goals up before the half time whistle – Gerry Mayes, Jock Cuthbertson and Bobby Nutley scoring. After the interval it was a drab affair, with Hibs content to hold onto their lead and St Bernards unconvincing in attack, and it was to be from a defensive mistake that they would gain their consolation goal. Hibs were to finish the season in 8th place, with St Bernards in 13th. Falkirk would win the title comfortable ahead of Dunfermline Athletic.

SATURDAY 31st MARCH 1923

80,000 fans were at Hampden to see if Hibs could lift the Scottish Cup for the third time, but instead it was Celtic who were victors and they lifted the cup for the 10th time. The conditions were excellent, the sides were well matched but Hibs did not manage to turn dominance into goals when they enjoyed their best spell of the game early in the second half, and fell behind to a Joe Cassidy goal in the 65th minute. Scottish International goalkeeper Willie Harper had been outstanding for Hibs in the tournament; indeed the final's only goal was the only goal he conceded in the entire tournament. Hibs' attack had been led by prolific goalscorer Jimmy McColl, who played against Hibs for Celtic in the 1914 final. This final saw both clubs managed by brothers – Hibs' boss was Alec Maley, while his big brother, Willie, managed Celtic. Two brothers would not go head-to – head like this in a Scottish Cup Final again until 1991.

HIBERNIAN FC
On This Day

APRIL

SATURDAY 1st APRIL 1995

Fans' favourite Mickey Weir had a bad April Fools' Day, coming on as a substitute only to be sent-off as Alex Miller's Hibs team was held to a 2-2 draw by Partick Thistle at Firhill in the league. Kevin Harper and Keith Wright scored for the Hibees, who had one eye on the following week's cup semi-final against Celtic at Ibrox. As a result of his sending off, Weir didn't feature in either of the cup games against Celtic.

SATURDAY 2nd APRIL 1983

Pat Stanton's Hibernian played host to relegation threatened Kilmarnock in the league. Hibs weren't enjoying the best of seasons either and went behind to a goal by Killie's Brian Gallagher. Stanton's men fought back and were 2-1 up at half-time. The Hibees then hit SIX goals in the second half to win the match 8-1, the first time the Hibees had scored eight in a league match since hammering Ayr Utd in late 1972, when Pat Stanton had been among the scorers. Hibs' goals in this rout of Killie came from Alan Gordon, Gordon Rae, Jackie McNamara and braces from Bobby Thomson and Willie Irvine. Young substitute Pat McCurdy also got on the score-sheet. Kilmarnock were relegated that season.

SUNDAY 2nd APRIL 2006

With neither side able to sell their full ticket allocation because of the SKY TV imposed Sunday lunch-time kick-off, 43,000 Hibs and Hearts fans were at Hampden to watch the Scottish Cup semi-final between the clubs. Hearts led 1-0 at half time thanks to a goal from Paul Hartley. Hibs had Ivan Sproule and Gary Smith red-carded in the second half, and two more goals from Hartley and a strike by Edgar Jankauskas crushed nine-man Hibs, who had been forced to field a weakened team because of injuries, suspensions and the departure of Garry O'Connor. It finished Hearts 4 Hibs 0.

WEDNESDAY 3rd APRIL 1963

Having been humbled 0-5 in Spain in the first leg of their Fairs Cup quarter-final against Valencia, Hibernian were really playing for pride in this second leg at Easter Road. Unable to overturn the huge deficit from the first leg, Hibs still managed a 2-1 win on the night against the Spanish giants, with goals from Gerry Baker and Tommy Preston. Hector Nunez scored for Valencia, who won the tie 6-2 on aggregate.

SATURDAY 3rd APRIL 1993

Neutral Tynecastle played host to this Scottish Cup semi-final between Hibs and Aberdeen. Hibs occupied the parts of Tynecastle where the Hearts support was usually housed, and Hearts' infamous 'shed' shook to the sound of 'Hail Hail'. Sadly for Hibs, Aberdeen won the fiercely contested match 1-0, thanks to Scott Booth's goal, and to a superb 'one man defence masterclass' performance by the Dons' Alex McLeish, a future Hibs manager, who seemed to get in the way of everything the Hibees threw at Aberdeen.

SATURDAY 3rd APRIL 1999

Alex McLeish's side faced Hamilton at their temporary home of Firhill in a division one match, looking to clinch the title and promotion to the SPL. Russell Latapy ran riot, scoring a goal in each half, both of which were superb strikes, to give Hibernian an easy 2-0 win and promotion back to their rightful place in Scotland's top flight. Latapy also had a second half penalty saved, but that mattered little to the Hibs fans, who made up most of the 4,300 crowd. A moving spectacle at the end saw the Hibs fans hold their scarves high to sing 'You'll Never Walk Alone', a popular song among the Hibernian support over the years until the early noughties. The Hibees were back!

SATURDAY 4th APRIL 1964

Having recently been poached from Dunfermline where he had worked miracles, new Hibs boss Jock Stein took charge of the team for the first time as the Hibees hosted Airdrieonians in the league. Hibs won the match 2-1, goals coming from Jim Scott and Neil Martin. The hype about Stein's arrival saw Hibs' gate increase to over 7,000 for this match, 2,000 more than at the previous home game against St Mirren.

SATURDAY 5th APRIL 1969

75,000 fans at Hampden saw Bob Shankly's men take on Jock Stein's formidable Celtic side in the League Cup Final. The final had been postponed from the previous October because of a bad fire at Hampden. Rampant Celtic annihilated Hibs, the Hoops having scored six goals without reply by the 73rd minute, including a Bobby Lennox hat-trick. Jimmy O'Rourke and Eric Stevenson scored late consolations for Hibs, to put a slightly more respectable slant on the scoreline for the Cabbage.

SATURDAY 5th APRIL 1986

Dens Park was the neutral venue as John Blackley's Hibs took on Aberdeen in the Scottish Cup semi-final, with an all Edinburgh final at stake, as Hearts were playing Dundee Utd in the other semi-final at Hampden. Hibs were looking for revenge for their League Cup Final defeat to The Dons earlier in the season, but didn't get it. Aberdeen won the match comfortably, 3-0, with goals from Billy Stark, Eric Black and Joe Miller. The Dons went on to beat Hearts in the Final by the same scoreline, only a week after Hearts had blown the league title at Dens Park in the 'Albert Kidd' game.

SATURDAY 5th APRIL 2003

At Rugby Park in the league, Bobby Williamson's Hibs team were humiliated, losing 6-2 to Williamson's old club, Kilmarnock. Mattias Jack and Ian Murray scored Hibs' consolation goals in what was truly an afternoon to forget for the Hibees in Ayrshire.

SATURDAY 6th APRIL 1985

John Blackley's Hibs side effectively secured their Premier League survival by beating fellow strugglers Dumbarton 2-0 at Boghead in front of just over 5,000 fans, Willie Irvine and Brian Rice netting for the Hibees. The two relegation spots were ultimately 'clinched' by Dumbarton and Morton.

FRIDAY 7th APRIL 1995

With Hampden closed for refurbishment, a green and white covered Ibrox was the venue for Hibs' Scottish Cup semi-final against Celtic, with an unusual Friday-night kick-off. The largely uneventful match ended nil-nil, with Celtic's Andy Walker having a penalty saved by Jim Leighton, meaning that the tie would have to be replayed at the same venue.

SATURDAY 8th APRIL 1944

Hibs made a scorching start in this Southern League Cup sectional tie, opening the scoring in 15 seconds through Gordon Smith, who was deftly supplied by Jimmy Nelson. Nelson was to have an impressive game, scoring a hat-trick to add to goals from wartime guest player Jimmy Caskie and Sammy Kean. Hibs eventually ran out winners by six goals to three. The result was good enough to win the group and Hibs progressed all the way to the final, where they were to lose to Rangers in cruel fashion.

SUNDAY 9th APRIL 2000

A 6pm kick-off and live SKY coverage meant that only 23,000 fans were at Hampden to see Hibs lose 1-2 to Aberdeen in the Scottish Cup semi-final. Russell Latapy had given Hibs the lead, but the Dons fought back to win the game, one of their goals coming from ex-Hibs man Andy Dow. Boss Alex McLeish's game plan was hampered when right-back Derek Collins limped-off early on, after having declared himself fit to play only a few hours earlier.

SATURDAY 9th APRIL 2005

Tony Mowbray's high flying Hibs side crashed out of the Scottish Cup at the semi-final stage, losing 1-2 to Dundee United at Hampden. Hibs took the lead with a Derek Riordan penalty early in the second half, but United hit back soon afterwards, with two goals in three minutes from Jim McIntrye and Jason Scotland.

SATURDAY 10th APRIL 1920

A keenly fought contest was witnessed by 6,000 fans against Morton at Cappielow, where Hibs managed to win a point against their high flying rivals. McAulay had put the home side ahead, but Hibs came roaring back, and were well worth their goal from Willie Stage and indeed could consider themselves unfortunate not to 'change ends' ahead in the match. Morton came more into the game, but such was the tenacity of the Hibernian defenders that the Cabbage rarely looked in trouble and indeed created the better scoring chances themselves. It ended 1-1. In the 22 team league, Hibs were to finish 18th, twelve places below Morton in 6th.

WEDNESDAY 11th APRIL 1979

Fewer than 10,000 fans attended the Scottish Cup semi-final between Hibs and Aberdeen. Aberdeen took the lead through Steve Archibald, but Gordon Rae equalised for the Hibees nine minutes later. An Ally McLeod penalty after 43 minutes made it 2-1 to Hibs at half-time and that's how the match finished.

TUESDAY 11th APRIL 1995

Ibrox was again the neutral venue, as Hibs and Celtic met to replay the Scottish Cup semi-final that they had drawn 0-0 the previous Friday. The winners would face Airdrieonians in the final. Hibs wore the purple and green away kit, while Celtic were in their usual hoops. Steven Tweed missed a sitter for Hibs, who were punished a few minutes later when Willie Falconer gave Celtic the lead. A sublime chip by John Collins put Celtic 2-0 up at the interval. Keith Wright pulled one back for Hibs after 66 minutes, but the Hoops sealed victory eight minutes from time with a Phil O'Donnell header.

SATURDAY 11th APRIL 1998

With Hibs, now managed by Alex McLeish, battling to avoid relegation, and Hearts going for the league title, the stakes were high for this derby at Easter Road. It was goal-less at half-time, then Barry 'Basher' Lavety gave Hibs the lead just on the hour mark. Hearts equalised ten minutes later, when John Robertson fired a stunning free-kick past Hibs 'keeper Bryan Gunn to level the match. Hibs got the winner on 80 minutes thanks to a sweet Kevin Harper strike. It finished Hibs 2 Hearts 1, effectively ending Hearts' title aspirations. The game also began Hibs' best run against Hearts of the last 30 years, Alex McLeish's team played Hearts 10 times and lost only once.

SATURDAY 12th APRIL 1975

Title-chasing Hibs thrashed Airdrieonians 6-1 at Easter Road in the league in front of just over 7,000 fans. Hibernian's goals came from Bobby Smith, Des Bremner, Arthur Duncan and a hat-trick from Joe Harper. Hibs finished runners-up in the title race that season, seven points behind champions Rangers and four points ahead of third placed Celtic.

SATURDAY 12th APRIL 1980

Eddie Turnbull's side were beaten 5-0 by Celtic at Hampden in the Scottish Cup semi-final, in front of 33,000 fans. This was Eddie Turnbull's last game in charge of Hibs. It was only 1-0 to Celtic at the break, but Hibs, despite having George Best, collapsed in the second half. Celtic's goals came from Lennox, Provan, Doyle, MacLeod and McAdam. The result of this match set up the now notorious 1980 Old Firm Cup Final, which ended in rioting.

WEDNESDAY 13th APRIL 2005

Inspired by late sub Amadou Konte, Hibs secured their first win over Hearts at Tynecastle of the 21st century. Hearts had taken the lead through Lee Miller after 40 minutes, but Konte's introduction after an hour changed the game. Garry O'Connor equalised after 68 minutes, and then Dean Shiels put Hibernian in front five minutes later. Tony Mowbray's men held on to win 2-1.

SATURDAY 13th APRIL 2013

Hibs returned to Hampden for a Scottish Cup semi-final against division one Falkirk. Falkirk's very young team ran riot in the first 30 minutes, going 3-0 up, causing some Hibs fans, who expected another collapse like the one against Hearts the previous season, to leave the stadium. Those fans missed one of the greatest fightbacks in Hibs' history. Whatever the manager said to the team at half-time did wonders, as Hibs came out and fought their way back to 3-3, with goals from Alex Harris, Leigh Griffiths and substitute Eoin Doyle. Griffiths even missed a penalty while it was still 3-2 in Falkirk's favour. Hibs dominated the second half and subsequent extra-time, with Griffiths netting the winner with just five minutes of extra-time left, taking Hibs through to the final 4-3 AET.

SATURDAY 14th APRIL 2001

Hibs faced runaway division one leaders Livingston at Hampden in the Scottish Cup semi-final. Alex McLeish's men took the lead after just two minutes through John O'Neil, and secured an easy win with further goals from O'Neil and Zitelli. The result was never in doubt and Hibs won 3-0. The loudest roar of the day came when Livi brought on former Hibs striker Darren Jackson, on loan from Hearts - it was a roar of derision. Victorious Hibs left the field with the fans' jubilant songs ringing in their ears, as the Hibees had reached their first Scottish Cup Final since 1979. They would play Celtic in the Final.

SATURDAY 14th APRIL 2012

Struggling in the league but improving, Hibs faced Aberdeen at Hampden in the Scottish Cup semi-final. Hibs took an early lead through Garry O'Connor, but that lead was cancelled out after an hour thanks to a stunning strike by the Dons' Rory Fallon. The match looked to be heading for extra-time, until Leigh Griffiths slotted the ball into the Aberdeen net with just five minutes remaining. Hibs won 2-1. It had been a close-run thing. Hibs would face either Celtic or Hearts in the Final.

WEDNESDAY 15th APRIL 1981

Bertie Auld's Hibs clinched the first division title and promotion by beating Clydebank 3-0 at Easter Road, with goals from Craig Paterson and a double from Arthur Duncan. The Hibees finished the season six points ahead of second placed Dundee, and Auld's team had a staggering goal-difference of plus-45. Dundee were promoted as runners-up. Hearts took Hibs place in the first division, having been relegated from the Premier League that season.

SUNDAY 15th APRIL 2007

Hibs faced Dunfermline Athletic in the Scottish Cup semi-final at Hampden, only days after a rumoured players' revolt against manager John Collins. Dunfermline had already disposed of Hearts and Rangers on their way to Hampden. The dull match ended 0-0 and would have to be decided by a replay. Before kick-off, Hibs fans voiced their support for the manager, as Hampden shook to the chant of "There's only one John Collins".

MONDAY 16th APRIL 1984

Hibernian legend Arthur Duncan made his final appearance for the club, going off injured with a broken collar-bone in the East of Scotland Shield Final against Meadowbank Thistle. The match finished 1-1 and went to penalties, with Meadowbank Thistle winning the shoot-out 5-4, to lift the minor-trophy at Easter Road.

SUNDAY 16th APRIL 1989

Alex Miller's Hibernian side was easily brushed aside by Celtic in the Scottish Cup semi-final at Hampden, losing three goals in the opening phase of the match. Tommy McIntyre, playing at right-back, was unable to cope with the pace of Celtic's young winger, Steve Fulton. Steve Archibald netted Hibs' consolation effort in the second half. Both sides wore black armbands for this match, in tribute to the 96 Liverpool fans who had been killed in the Hilsborough Disaster the day before.

SATURDAY 17th APRIL 1993

Hibs hosted Celtic in the league, who were in turmoil off the park and sported a strange black and jade kit for the game. Hibs were 2-0 up inside seven minutes, with goals from Keith Wright and Gareth Evans, and then went three up before the interval thanks to a Darren Jackson penalty. Alex Miller told the team to protect the lead in the second half, which they did easily, asides from a Celtic consolation goal by veteran striker Charlie Nicholas. Hibs fans spent most of the game goading the visiting support, not about their financial plight, but simply about how bad their team was.

SATURDAY 18th APRIL 1981

Hibs played their final home game of the 1980-81 season in the old first division, having been relegated the previous season. Manager Bertie Auld had won promotion for the Cabbage at the first attempt, Hibs going up as Division One champions, eventually finishing six points ahead of runners-up Dundee. Just 8,000 fans were at this penultimate match of the season, in which Hibs beat Raith Rovers 2-0 thanks to goals from Ralph Callachan and Gary Murray. The Hibees were back!

SATURDAY 18th APRIL 1998

Relegation threatened Hibs were running out of games in which to save themselves from the drop, despite a vast improvement under Alex McLeish. The Hibees went to East End Park to play fellow strugglers Dunfermline. 8,000 Hibbies crossed The Forth for this vital match. Hibs played well, roared on by the huge travelling support, but Grant Brebner, otherwise a hero of Hibs' fightback towards the end of the season, scored a second half own goal. Hibs pressed and pressed the Pars, the Hibs fans willing the ball into the net, and in the fifth minute of injury time defender Brian Welsh rose to head a Kevin Harper corner into the net, the game finishing 1-1. It was still a tall-order, but the belief Hibs showed in this game, and in the weeks before it, made many Hibs fans think that against all odds, Hibernian could do the unthinkable, they could stay up. The question was – would they?

WEDNESDAY 19th APRIL 1961

Hibernian faced AS Roma at Easter Road in the UEFA Cup semi-final first leg in front of 35,000 fans. Joe Baker and Johnny Macleod scored for the Cabbage either side of Lojacono's double for Roma, the match ending 2-2 on the night, with a mouth-watering second leg in the Eternal City now on the cards.

SATURDAY 20th APRIL 1946

The final season of wartime football was coming to an end as Hibs and Dundee played out this first round, first leg, Victory Cup tie in front of 18,000 at Easter Road. Hibs won comfortably by 3-0, the goals all coming from winger Gordon Smith who completed his hat-trick in the 70th minute. Whilst Hibs had not been at their best, they still created a number of chances that Bennett in the Dundee goal did well to stop. Hibs safely saw out the game at Dens Park, losing 2-0 to advance 3-2 on aggregate.

SATURDAY 21st APRIL 1979

Hibs ran up their biggest score of the season thus far, by hammering Motherwell 4-0 at Easter Road with goals from Gordon Rae, Ralph Callachan, Des Bremner and Colin Campbell. Hibs' 17 year-old striker Steve Brown had seven attempts on target without scoring. The result left Motherwell rooted to the bottom of the league.

SATURDAY 22nd APRIL 2000

Hibs were at Parkhead on league business, chasing a possible UEFA Cup spot. Stuart Lovell gave Hibs the lead after 30 minutes and Alex McLeish's men held onto the lead until the 79th minute, Stephane Mahe levelling for Celtic. The draw meant that Rangers had won the title with five games to spare. Five Hibs players were booked in this match, despite it not being a dirty game. Celtic fans spent most of the match berating their Dutch flop Regi Blinker.

SATURDAY 23rd APRIL 1910

Hibs prevailed against Motherwell in a league game played at Easter Road, in front of a small crowd of about a thousand. A strong wind interfered with the play, but the away side attempted some nice football and nearly took the lead, but the home goalkeeper was up to the task. Willie Smith gave Hibernian a lead at half time, and it was not one they were to relinquish. Hibs were on top in the second half, but it was nearing the end of the game when they gave the Motherwell goalkeeper some 'ticklish' shots to save. It ended 1-0 to Hibs.

MONDAY 24th APRIL 1972

Turnbull's Tornadoes defeated Rangers 2-0 at Hampden in the Scottish Cup semi-final replay, in a game watched by around 58,000 fans. Hibs' goals came courtesy of Pat Stanton in the first half and Alex Edwards in the second. The first game nine days earlier had ended 1-1, future Hearts boss Alex MacDonald scoring for the 'Gers, Jimmy O'Rourke equalising for the Hibees, in front of over 75,000 fans. Hibs would face Celtic in the Final.

TUESDAY 24th APRIL 2007

Hibs blew their chances of winning both of Scotland's major cup competitions in the same season, as they lost their Scottish Cup semi-final replay to Dunfermline Athletic at Hampden Park in front of barely 7,000 fans. Jim McIntyre scored the only goal of the game with a coolly taken late penalty in the match's closing minutes, meaning that the Easter Road men would have to be happy with winning only one trophy that season. The scanty crowd at this match persuaded the SFA to do away with replays at the semi-final stage of the tournament.

SATURDAY 25th APRIL 1953

Hibs thumped Third Lanark 7-1 at Easter Road, with Bobby Johnstone bagging a hat-trick. The 15,000 fans at the game had events elsewhere on their minds, as Aberdeen were playing Rangers in the Scottish Cup Final on the same day. A huge roar went around Easter Road when Aberdeen equalised to take the match to a replay, as many fans were listening to the final on portable radios. As Third Lanark had narrowly lost the semi-final to Rangers, there weren't many people at Easter Road supporting the Govan side that day.

SATURDAY 25th APRIL 1998

Battling relegation, Alex McLeish's rejuvenated side faced an away match in the league against title-chasing Celtic. Hibs players stated their intent not to lose by linking arms at the centre-circle to 'face-down' the Celtic players' famous pre-match huddle before kick-off. What followed can be best described as an intense midfield battle, or in layman's terms, a dull kicking-match. There were only two goal attempts in the entire game, Hibs brilliantly stopping Celtic and gaining the 0-0 draw that they had obviously been aiming for in their fight for survival. Boss Alex McLeish and Celtic's assistant Murdo MacLeod were both sent to the stand after 'handbags' on the touchline, such was the importance of the match to both teams, for very different reasons.

SATURDAY 26th APRIL 1902

Hibs won the Scottish Cup for the second time, and in doing so became the last team to win the cup at the home of their opponents. The final had originally been scheduled to take place at Ibrox a fortnight earlier, but on 5th April the Western Tribune stand collapsed during the Annual Scotland and England game, killing 25 people and injuring 517. Hibernian agreed to play at Parkhead instead, as they felt "no first class team need fear playing on the first class pitch there." The final was evenly contested and while Celtic may have had the better of the early exchanges, the Scottish international goalkeeper Harry Rennie was a match for them. Hibs came more into the game, and it was in the 75th minute that Andy McGeachan headed the winning goal.

WEDNESDAY 26th APRIL 1961

Hibs travelled to Rome to play AS Roma in their UEFA Cup semi-final second leg, the first leg having ended 2-2. Another exciting match saw the Hibees 3-1 up by the midway point of the second half and heading for the Final, but the Italian masters dug in and pegged it back to 3-3. Hibs' goals came from Bobby Kinloch and a double from the great Joe Baker, while Roma's goals came from a double by Manfredini and another goal by Lojacono. Because back then there was no away-goals rule, and indeed no penalty shoot-outs or extra-time, the match was to go to a single replay at a neutral venue. Dubious decisions and intrigue behind the scenes meant that the 'neutral' venue was... Rome.

WEDNESDAY 27th APRIL 1921

Hibs rounded off their 42 game league campaign with a 2-0 victory over Scottish Cup winners Partick Thistle in front of around 5,000 spectators. Several members of Particks' cup winning team were absent, whilst Hibs gave a debut to promising junior Jimmy Buchanan. Hibs were enterprising in the first half, but Partick came into play the more the game went on and at half-time the scores were still level. In the second half, the home team were much better and scored goals from Hugh Shaw and Davie Anderson – both from headers.

MONDAY 28th APRIL 1941

In this rearranged derby game at Tynecastle Hibs triumphed over a full strength Hearts side by 5-3. Hibs had played two junior trialists, 16-year-old Gordon Smith, and 17-year-old Bobby Combe – Gordon would mark his debut with a hat-trick, whilst Bobby also scored in the victory. Hearts had lined up Gordon for a trial, but Hibs manager Willie McCartney persuaded the youngster that he would be signed after the game, and he chose Hibs over his boyhood heroes. Between them, Smith and Combe would go onto play over 1,000 games for Hibs, scoring 400 goals.

SATURDAY 29th APRIL 1933

The Hibernians, as they were then known, concluded their two year exile in the lower division by taking a point from Station Park against Forfar Athletic. The league was already won, and Hibs did not play their strongest side. In front of around 1,500 fans Hibs took the lead on three separate occasions and were pegged back with equalising goals each time. It ended 3-3. Paddy Connolly notched all the Hibs goals, his only hat- trick for the Easter Road side. Better known for his decade of service to Celtic, Connolly never played for Hibs again and left for Airdrieonians in the summer.

SATURDAY 30th APRIL 2005

Hibs hadn't won at Celtic Park since 1992, but the 13-year hoodoo came to an end in style in this league match. Celtic were chasing the title and were stunned when Garry O'Connor gave Hibs the lead after just six minutes. Craig Beattie equalised for Celtic on the hour. Both sides missed several scoring chances in between the first two goals. The home crowd's thunderous roars in the second half didn't unnerve the yellow-clad Hibees and recent signing Ivan Sproule put Hibs 2-1 up with just 11 minutes remaining. Celtic were stunned two minutes later when a cool chip from Scott Brown put Hibernian 3-1 up, and despite late pressing by the hosts, that's how it finished. The only disappointment for Tony Mowbray's side, and Hibs fans, was knowing that they would have been facing Celtic in the Scottish Cup Final a few weeks later, fully capable of beating the Glasgow giants, if it wasn't for Hibs' semi-final defeat to Dundee Utd earlier in the month.

SATURDAY 30th APRIL 2011

Hibernian's greatest, Eddie Turnbull, died aged 88 from a respiratory illness. As a player he played in all three of Scotland's games at the 1958 World-Cup in Sweden, and played 487 games for Hibs, scoring an incredible 202 goals between 1946 and 1959. During his playing career at Hibs he won three League Championships. As Hibs manager, he won just one League Cup and two Drybrough Cups, but was still immensely successful as boss, beating Hearts 7-0 in 1973 and guiding Hibs to two second-place league finishes, as well as several cup finals. As both a player and a manager, he was involved in Hibernian's greatest European matches. Turnbull was, and is, simply the greatest Hibernian. Hibs lost 2-1 at home to St Johnstone in the league on the day he died.

HIBERNIAN FC
On This Day

MAY

SATURDAY 1st MAY 1965

Bob Shankly's Hibernian defeated local rivals Hearts 3-0 at Easter Road in front of just over 13,000 fans, to lift the Summer Cup. Hibs' goals came courtesy of Jim Scott and a brace from Neil Martin. The Summer Cup may sound like an obscure trophy now, but back then in the days of little or no televised or foreign football coverage it was a prestigious cup to win, as was the Drybrough Cup. Most fans in bygone days only cared about the Scottish game.

SATURDAY 2nd MAY 1992

The final day of the 1991/92 league season saw Hibs travel to Celtic Park. Alex Miller's men had already won the League Cup, qualifying for the UEFA Cup by doing so, and had been unluckily eliminated from the other cup at the quarter-final stage. A relaxed Hibs earned a deserved victory, taking the lead through an early Derek Whyte own-goal, then doubling the lead through Pat McGinlay after 64 minutes. Steve Fulton scored a late consolation for Celtic. Celtic's Paul McStay threw his jersey into the 'jungle' as a farewell to the Celtic fans, as he was rumoured to be leaving, but he actually didn't leave. As for Hibs, their win secured them a fifth place league finish, it also ensured that Hearts finished as runners-up, so both Edinburgh sides would compete in Europe the following season.

SATURDAY 2nd MAY 1998

Hibs lost 1-2 at home to Dundee United and were relegated from the Scottish Premier League, despite a revival in fortunes since the appointment of Alex McLeish as manager that had almost saved them from the drop. Two goals from Kjel Olafsson were enough to sink Hibs, despite Grant Brebner managing to keep the fight for survival alive by scoring for Hibs.

SATURDAY 3rd MAY 1980

There was a happy Hibee at Easter Road named Gordon Strachan, but he was about the only one, as already relegated Hibs, under Willie Ormond, were thrashed 0-5 by a rampant Aberdeen side whose team included the wee Hibs fan. Ormond had been in temporary charge of Hibs after Eddie Turnbull resigned following Hibs' 5-0 drubbing in the Scottish Cup semi-final a few weeks before. Hibs 'keeper

Dave Huggins made his debut in this match, and never played for the club again.

SATURDAY 3rd MAY 1986

A crowd of just under 4,000 at Easter Road watched Hibs lose 1-2 to Dundee United, Hibs' goal coming from Steve Cowan. Many fans at the game were listening to another match on the radio, some Hibs players were even shouting to the fans on the terracing, asking them what the score was in that game. The other game in question was at Dens Park, where Hearts only need a draw to win the League Title, and were drawing 0-0. Even if Hearts didn't manage a draw, their nearest challengers, Celtic, needed to win by five goals in order to snatch the title from the Jambos on goal-difference. As you can imagine, there was elation at Easter Road when news filtered through that Celtic had thrashed St Mirren 5-0 at Love Street, and that with just seven minutes to go, Dundee substitute Albert Kidd had netted twice against Hearts, robbing them of the title. Dundee won 2-0. Albert Kidd has since become a cult-hero in Scottish football to fans of both Hibs and Celtic. In those days, before live televised games, when Hibs played one Dundee team at home, Hearts played the other one away, and vice versa. The same 'rule' applied when Hibs and Hearts played Celtic and Rangers. Hearts went on to also lose the Scottish Cup Final 0-3 to Aberdeen the following week.

TUESDAY 3rd MAY 1994

The last ever match at Easter Road where fans stood on terracing saw the Hibees welcome Rangers, who could win the league by avoiding defeat in the game. Hibs won the match 1-0 thanks to a Keith Wright header, spoiling the 'party' for the visiting fans a little, though results elsewhere that night meant that they secured the title anyway, despite losing. Though Hibs had one more home game to play against Kilmarnock that season, the east terracing was closed for that game while seats were added to it, so, the last memory many Hibs fans have of standing on terracing at Easter Road is of bouncing up and down while singing 'can you hear the Rangers sing?' after beating the Govan side.

SATURDAY 4th MAY 1946

Over 40,000 fans crammed into Tynecastle for this second round Victory Cup tie, and it was Willie McCartney who again worked his magic to see the green and white team prevail over their oldest rivals. Tommy Walker had returned to the maroons, but his presence was not enough to inspire a victory. Hibs had to re-shuffle their side after injuries to Finnigan and Kean at Parkhead the previous Wednesday. Hibs won through in the end in a fast paced game by 3-1, the goals scored by Jock Weir(2) and Willie Peat.

WEDNESDAY 5th MAY 2010

Hibs put six goals past Motherwell at Fir Park in one of the most remarkable matches in Scottish football history. Colin Nish scored a hat-trick, Anthony Stokes scored two and Derek Riordan scored one. Unfortunately for John Hughes' team, Motherwell also scored six! Hibs were 4-2 up at half-time, then went 6-2 up in the second half, only for Motherwell to bag another four goals, meaning the match finished 6-6!

SATURDAY 6th MAY 1972

106,000 fans crammed into Hampden for the Scottish Cup Final between Hibernian and Celtic. Scotland's two greatest managers of the day, Eddie Turnbull and Jock Stein, both picked attacking sides. Celtic took the lead in the second minute through Billy McNeil but Alan Gordon equalised ten minutes later. The Hibees competed well until Dixie Deans scored the first goal of his hat-trick, after 23 minutes. Two late goals by Celtic's Lou Macari completed the rout, the game finishing Hibs 1 Celtic 6. Hibs would not have to wait very long for revenge, as they played Celtic in the League Cup Final later that year.

SATURDAY 6th MAY 1995

Just under 8,000 fans were at Easter Road for the final Edinburgh derby of the season, as both 'ends' behind the goals were undergoing demolition, reducing the stadium capacity temporarily. Hearts took the lead midway through the first half through former Rangers striker David Hagen, but the Hibees ran out 3-1 winners, thanks to three goals in ten second half minutes from Mickey Weir, Keith Wright and

Kevin Harper. Hibs won three out of the four derbies that season, prior to that season, Hearts had been unbeaten in the fixture since early 1989.

SUNDAY 6th MAY 2001

Champions Celtic were the visitors to Easter Road for a league match which was a dress-rehearsal for the upcoming Scottish Cup Final between the sides. Hibs had injury problems so striker Dirk Lehmann played in central-defence. Hibs competed well and had several chances, but were ultimately ripped apart by Martin O'Neil's side, who took the lead in the fourth minute through Jackie McNamara, who then doubled Celtic's lead after 18 minutes. The second half was no different as Larsson, Stubbs and Moravcik had Celtic 5-0 up by the 80th minute. Alan Stubbs' goal was a header, after he had come on as a substitute for his first appearance in months, following serious illness. On-loan striker Marc Libra scored two late consolation goals for the Hibees to make the scoreline slightly less embarrassing and it finished Hibs 2 Celtic 5, a grim warning for what was to unfold in the upcoming Cup Final.

SATURDAY 7th MAY 1988

The last game of the 1987/88 season saw already relegated Morton visit Easter Road. In glorious sunshine, Hibs beat the Greenock side 3-1, but the match is best remembered not for the result, but for the fact that Hibs' 'keeper Andy Goram scored directly from a clearance from his own box. Going 'down the slope', Goram's powerful kick sailed over the heads of the outfield players and bounced on the penalty spot and over the helpless Morton 'keeper David Wylie into the net, Wylie indignantly scrambling after it after realising that he had mistimed his rush from goal to get the ball, and eventually falling into the net himself. Hibs' other goals came from Neil Orr and Joe Tortolano. Many Hibbies believed that they would never see a Hibs goalie score like that again.

THURSDAY 7th MAY 2009

Mixu Paatelainen's Hibs side went to Tynecastle for the final Edinburgh Derby of the season, with a depleted squad ravaged by injuries and suspensions. Talk in the media before the game was about how many goals Hibs would lose by, and many Hearts fans thought that against this weakened Hibs team, they would finally be able to emulate Hibs' famous seven-goal victory in the same fixture at the same ground. Hearts, and much of the media, were left with egg on their faces, as Hibs won the match 1-0 thanks to a late Derek Riordan penalty, much to the delight of the small but noisy Hibs support in the Roseburn Stand, and those watching the game live on Setanta. Several young Hearts fans invaded the pitch in an attempt to assault Riordan after his goal, one of the pitch invaders managing to punch himself in the face. The fan was later banned from Tynecastle.

SATURDAY 8th MAY 1999

A near capacity crowd at Easter Road saw Alex McLeish and his already promoted team officially presented with the division one trophy, as they hosted runners-up Falkirk. Hibs had already clinched the title and promotion a month earlier. Scott Crabbe's quest for a goal against Hibs was thwarted early on, when his penalty was brilliantly saved by Hibs 'keeper Ollie Gottskalksson. Russell Latapy and Franck Sauzee, fast becoming cult-heroes among Hibs fans, then gave the Hibees the lead when Latapy rolled a free-kick to the big Frenchman, who unleashed a trademark 40-yard screamer into the 'postage stamp' corner of the net at the Hibs end of the ground. Paul Hartley doubled Hibs' lead in the second half, finishing off a fine move. Crabbe did eventually get a goal, but his consolation strike for the Bairns didn't spoil the party. Hibernian were back! There was a good-natured pitch invasion from the delighted fans, and Paul Hartley ran around like an excited schoolboy celebrating, until his team-mates hoisted the youngster high from the ground together. Most moving perhaps, was the joy on the faces of club legends Pat McGinlay and John Hughes, who had been in tears just a year ago when the club had been relegated, and had, somewhat harshly, blamed themselves. What a difference a year makes! Hibs won the title by 23 points – a record at that time.

SATURDAY 9th MAY 1998

Already relegated Hibs played the final match of the 1997/98 season against Kilmarnock at Rugby Park. A typical end of season affair ended in a 1-1 draw, Stevie Crawford scoring for Hibs, in front of a crowd of over 12,000!

DEREK RIORDAN WITH A STUNNING STRIKE AGAINST HEARTS

SATURDAY 10th MAY 1919

Hibs rounded off a wretched season with a 3-3 draw at Airdrie. Hibs finished bottom of 18 teams, and were saved from relegation by the lack of a second tier in the years after the war. Davy Gordon's side won just five of their league games all season, but they had looked on course for the two points in this game as they had dominated the first half, and the early part of the second too, as they raced into a three goal lead through goals from Bobby Gilmour(2) and Jimmy Williamson. Airdrie had other ideas, and pulled back the deficit, and Hibs were left to hang on for a point in the closing stages.

SATURDAY 11th MAY 1985

Just over 7,000 fans at Easter Road saw Hibs beat Rangers 1-0 in the season's final league match, Paul Kane scoring for John Blackley's men. Hibs didn't play great, but Rangers were woeful. It had been a largely disappointing season for both teams, but that was put into perspective as the day wore on, as news filtered through to Scotland about the Bradford City Fire at Valley Parade that day, which had killed 56 fans and injured almost 300 more.

FRIDAY 12th MAY 1950

It sounds unlikely now, but once upon a time Hibs visited Bayern Munich to play a friendly, and left having won 6-1. The Germans may not have been the force that they are now, but Hans Bauer went onto to lift the World Cup in 1954 with West Germany after facing Hibs. Hibs dominated the friendly, and ran out easy winners. Goals were scored by Gordon Smith(2), Lawrie Reilly, Jimmy Souness and Willie Ormond. Jimmy Souness was unfortunate in that his best performances always seemed to come in friendlies and he was unable to break into the team by displacing any of the Famous Five. A product of George Heriot's school, he was also good enough to play cricket for Scotland.

WEDNESDAY 13th MAY 1964

Over 10,000 fans turned up at Easter Road to see Hibs beat Hearts 1-0 in the Summer Cup, the only trophy which manager Jock Stein won during his regrettably short spell in the Easter Road hot-seat. Hibs scored through Stan Vincent.

SATURDAY 14th MAY 2011

Derek Riordan played his last ever match for Hibernian, scoring after 21 minutes for Colin Calderwood's men. Sadly, Aberdeen scored three goals in the second half to win 3-1, taking all three points back up north. During Riordan's two spells at Hibs he scored 104 goals in 260 appearances, many of those goals being 'screamers'. This match saw Hibs and Aberdeen fans perform a minute's applause in honour of Eddie Turnbull, a legend at both clubs, who had recently died.

SATURDAY 15th MAY 2004

A visit to Almondvale on the final day of the league season saw Hibs, under interim boss Gerry McCabe, thrashed 4-1 by Livingston. Matt Doumbe scored Hibs' consolation. Under-fire boss Bobby Williamson had stepped down a few weeks before. Hibs played the West Lothian side five times that season, losing four times, including in the League Cup Final.

SATURDAY 16th MAY 1953

'Hibs completely kings of the Castle' proclaimed one newspaper as the Hibees comfortably saw off Newcastle United in this Coronation Cup semi-final at Ibrox in front of 35,000 fans. Eddie Turnbull and Lawrie Reilly scored first half goals to put Hibs in command, and it was more of the same after the break when Bobby Johnstone and Eddie Turnbull strikes gave Hibs a decisive 4-0 victory. Newcastle had earlier missed a first half penalty which may have changed the course of the game. Ronnie Simpson was in goals for Newcastle on this day, and he was to move to Hibs later in his career, before joining Celtic and both winning the European Cup and being capped in his late thirties.

SATURDAY 17th MAY 1997

Jim Duffy had managed to guide Hibs to second bottom of the league in this season, after taking over while Hibernian were still mid-table. This meant that Hibs now faced a two-legged relegation play off against Airdrieonians in order to see who would play in the Premier League the next season. In this first leg at Easter Road, Hibs won 1-0 , thanks to an own-goal by Airdrie's Steve Cooper. The second leg would be played at Airdrie's temporary home, Broadwood, in Cumbernauld. This was Gordon Hunter's last game for Hibs, as he was sent-off, so Hibs would be without him for the second leg at Broadwood.

SATURDAY 18th MAY 1963

In a season best remembered for atrocious weather and many matches being postponed, Walter Galbraith's side thumped Raith Rovers 4-0 at Starks Park on the last day, goals coming from John Fraser, Gerry Baker and a double by John Baxter. Raith finished bottom and were relegated with a pathetic final tally of just NINE points. Mind you, Hibs weren't exactly strong finishers either, ending the season third from bottom with just 25 points, narrowly avoiding the drop themselves by finishing two points above second bottom Clyde, who were also relegated.

SATURDAY 19th MAY 2012

Having been brought in simply to save what was the departed Colin Calderwood's awful Hibs team from relegation, Pat Fenlon had also somehow managed to guide his hastily assembled squad of mostly loan players at Hibs, not only to SPL survival, but also to the Scottish Cup Final, where they faced city-rivals Hearts. Hibs' shoestring-budget squad was no match for that of big-spending Hearts on paper, yet was holding its own in the Final, battling away, 1-2 down at half-time. Referee Craig Thomson, a Hearts fan, ruined the match as a contest just after the interval, awarding Hearts a penalty and sending of Hibs defender Pa Kujabi for a foul that was clearly outside the box, though his second yellow card was deserved. Hearts scored the penalty and Hibs collapsed, losing the biggest derby in years, 1-5. James McPake had netted Hibs' only goal just before half-time. Hearts never managed to score seven, though.

SUNDAY 20th MAY 2007

The final day of the 2006/07 season at Easter Road saw John Collins' side beat the league champions. 0-0 at half-time, Celtic then took the lead through former Hibee Derek Riordan after 56 minutes, but Scott Brown, in his last game for Hibs, equalised with a flying header just four minutes later. It was an exciting game, which Hibs eventually won 2-1 when Ivan Sproule, also playing the last game of his first spell at Hibs, rounded Celtic's 'keeper in the last minute to score the winner. It was a terrific way to end the season for Hibs, but beating Celtic the week before their Scottish Cup Final against Dunfermline left many fans again wondering 'what might have

TERRY BUTCHER FOLLOWING ANOTHER DIFFICULT HIBS PERFORMANCE

been', had Hibs beaten the Pars in the Scottish Cup semi-final and been facing Celtic in the Final. Hibs could have done the cup-double that season, but in the end, had to make do with just one cup.

THURSDAY 21st MAY 1981

One of the oddest matches in the club's history saw Bertie Auld's Hibs team play a friendly in Port-au-Prince, Haiti, against Haiti's national side, such as it was. Hibs lost the match 0-1!

WEDNESDAY 21st MAY 2014

In free-fall for months with abysmal form, Hibs, under Terry Butcher, had spiralled downward in the second half of the season and ended up finishing second bottom, and thus faced a two-legged play-off against Championship side Hamilton Accies, who had recently beaten Morton 10-0 in a league match, amid what was for them a good end of season spurt. With Hibs' Premiership status in danger, a loud support roared on the Hibees at New Douglas Park. Hibs won this first leg 2-0, with a goal in each half from young striker Jason Cummings, and it looked like Hibs had merely to finish the job in the second leg at Easter Road.

THURSDAY 22nd MAY 1997

Broadwood Stadium hosted the second leg of Hibs' relegation play-off against Airdrieonians. Hibs were defending a one goal lead from the first leg, but blew that when Airdrie scored in the first minute. Steve Cooper then missed a penalty for Airdrie midway through the first half, having insisted on taking the kick himself to make amends for his OG in the first leg. Airdrie were all over Hibs, but Hibs held on until half-time, 0-1 down. Airdrie's rough style of play was their undoing in the second half, as Darren Jackson scored two penalties for Hibs, one right after the re-start, the second on 70 minutes. Paul Tosh then scored for Hibs with eight minutes remaining, then substitute Keith Wright put Hibs 4-1 up on the night just one minute later. In the closing stages, Jimmy Sandison was sent-off for Airdrie and Kenny Black pulled one back for the Diamonds, with the game's fourth penalty. It finished 4-2 to Hibs on the night, 5-2 on aggregate, meaning Hibs had retained their top-flight status. The second half performance was inspired by Hibs' old guard of Leighton, Jackson,

Wright and McGinlay, all but one of whom would leave the club in the summer. Despite survival, there were worrying signs for fans of Jim Duffy's side.

SUNDAY 22nd MAY 2005

The final league game of the season saw Tony Mowbray's side welcome Rangers to Easter Road. Hibs were looking to qualify for the UEFA Cup, while Rangers were aiming to pip Celtic to the title, needing a win for themselves and also needing Celtic to lose at Fir Park. Hibs went out to win the game and secure that European place, missing several chances, but then Gary Caldwell deflected a Nacho Novo effort into his own net after 60 minutes to put the 'Gers 1-0 up. As it stood after Novo's goal, with Hearts also beating Hibs' Euro challengers Aberdeen, the score at Easter Road suited both sides, and the game petered out into a half-hearted training exercise for the final 30 minutes, neither side really trying. As it happened, Celtic lost two late goals at Motherwell and thus Rangers won the title at Easter Road, as the game finished 1-0 to Rangers, also meaning that Hibs had finished third and qualified for Europe. Some over excited Hibs fans invaded the pitch, while others left the stadium with mixed emotions following the farce of the game's last 30 minutes, delighted with third place, not so happy at hosting another team's title party.

SATURDAY 23rd MAY 1964

Amid glorious sunshine, Hibernian defeated Dunfermline Athletic 3-1 at neutral Tynecastle in front of 14,000 fans in a Summer Cup group play-off decider. Hibs' goals came from Stan Vincent and a double from Jim Scott.

SATURDAY 24th MAY 2003

Just under 10,000 fans were at Easter Road for the final league game of the season against Partick Thistle. A somewhat exciting match saw Bobby Williamson's men take the lead through a Mathias Jack header. Thistle equalised through veteran Gerry Britton, but Hibs were 2-1 up at half-time thanks to a goal from Scott Brown. David Rowson equalised for the 'Jags seven minutes into the second half, and both sides missed chances aplenty, before Thistle's other veteran forward, Alex 'toastie' Burns, nodded in the winner three minutes from time to make it Hibs 2 Partick Thistle 3 in the end. Chic Charnley came on as late substitute for Thistle, in what was to be his last top-flight game, and was applauded by both sets of fans.

SUNDAY 25th MAY 2014

Terry Butcher's Hibernian took on Hamilton in the second leg of the relegation play-off. Hibs were 2-0 up from the first leg, but had not been performing well at home since the closure of the old East Stand back in 2010. Jason Scotland put Hamilton 1-0 up after 12 minutes, and the 'Accies players could smell the fear inside Easter Road. Unbelievably, Terry Butcher started the game with just one up-front, and then in the latter stages took OFF striker Paul Heffernan and replaced him with a midfielder, having already taken off winger Alex Harris, who himself had come on as an early substitute for the injured Danny Haynes. Butcher chose to try to defend Hibs' slim one-goal advantage, and it backfired spectacularly when Hamilton, always the better team, grabbed an injury time equaliser through Tony Andreu to take the play-off into extra-time, which yielded no further goals, the tie finishing 2-2 on aggregate after 120 minutes. Hibs lost the penalty-shoot out 4-3, Jason Cummings and Kevin Thomson having their kicks saved, meaning that Hibs went down, Hamilton went up. Hibs had been seventh in the league when Pat Fenlon had left in early November 2013, nowhere near the relegation zone, but the 'limbo' period with Jimmy Nichol at the helm and then Butcher's disastrous spell in charge got Hibs relegated. Butcher is, statistically, the worst manager in Hibernian's history.

SATURDAY 26th MAY 2001

Hibs travelled to Hampden where they faced treble-chasing Celtic in the Scottish Cup Final. Hibs were without talismanic midfielder Russell Latapy because of his fall-out with the manager. A woeful display by the Easter Road men saw them lose 0-3 to Martin O'Neil's very strong, physical team, whose scorers were Jackie McNamara and Henrik Larsson(2). Striker Tom McManus was left out of the Hibs squad, despite having scored in every other round other than the semi-final.

SUNDAY 26th MAY 2013

Manager Pat Fenlon guided Hibs to their second consecutive Scottish Cup Final, his side having battled and bulldozed all opposition in previous rounds. Star striker Leigh Griffiths was carrying an injury, but played. Unfortunately for Hibs, they found themselves in much the same position as they had been in the 2001 Final – facing a very strong, hungry Celtic side. An early header from striker Eoin Doyle was Hibs' only real chance in the game. Hooper gave Celtic ninth minute lead, then he doubled Neil Lennon's side's advantage on 30 mins. Hibs competed well but were simply outplayed, Joe Ledley's goal on 80 minutes made the match sound more one-sided than it actually was, and though they lost 3-0, Hibs players and fans alike could leave the stadium with their heads held high.

SATURDAY 27th MAY 1961

Hibs' UEFA Cup semi-final replay ended in a heavy defeat, Roma thrashing Hibs 6-0 to progress to the Final. Whatever went on behind the scenes regarding this match and where it was played is still debated by Hibs fans to this day. Roma's suspiciously easy victory came courtesy of four goals from Manfredini and a strike apiece for Menichelli and Selmosson. Roma won the two-legged final 4-2 on aggregate, beating Birmingham City. Had things been different, this tournament would have had a 'battle of Britain' Final.

MONDAY 28th MAY 1979

After two goal-less draws, Hibs took on Rangers in the Scottish Cup Final at Hampden, looking to win the second replay. Hibs lost the third and final game 3-2, Rangers' winning goal coming from an own-goal by Hibs' Arthur Duncan. 50,000 fans had watched the first match, barely 30,000 were there to see the tie finally decided in the third.

SATURDAY 29th MAY 1943

The Hibs manager Willie McCartney sympathised with Partick Thistle on this day, after they had been crushed 7-0 by a rampant Hibs side in this Summer Cup first round first-leg game. Hibs were imperious and irresistible, and once they had broken the resilience of the Partick defence in the first half hour they dominated the rest of the game. Doubles from Bobby Baxter and Jock Cuthbertson put Hibs four up by half-time, and Willie Anderson put Hibs five ahead shortly before going off injured with 35 minutes remaining. Playing with ten men didn't prove to be too much of a hurdle and Gordon Smith added a double in the last ten minutes. Hibs also won the return leg at Firhill, 5-2, with Charles McGilvray scoring a hat-trick on a rare outing for Hibs.

SATURDAY 30th MAY 1964

The second leg of Hibs' Summer Cup semi-final against Kilmarnock at Easter Road saw 18,000 fans turn up in glorious sunshine. 3-4 down from the first leg at Rugby Park, Jock Stein's Hibees easily brushed aside the Ayrshire men in Edinburgh, winning 3-0, thanks to a first-half strike by Stan Vincent and a goal in each half from Neil Martin, to give Hibs a 6-4 aggregate win.

THURSDAY 31st MAY 1979

Just three days after losing the Scottish Cup Final to Rangers, after TWO replays, Eddie Turnbull's side played host to the Glasgow side in the last league game of the season. Typically, having just lost to them in the Cup Final, Hibs went out and beat Rangers 2-1, with goals from Ally Brazil and Gordon Rae. Only 3,300 fans attended this match.

HIBERNIAN FC
On This Day

JUNE

THURSDAY 1st JUNE 1978

On an end of season tour of Canada, Eddie Turnbull's Hibs team thrashed Ottawa Tigers 7-0. The same tour saw Hibernian play against another six top Canadian teams, drawing twice and winning four times. Including the game against Ottawa, Hibs scored 36 goals in the tour's seven games, conceding just four.

SUNDAY 2nd JUNE 1968

With a tour of North America cancelled, Bob Shankly's Hibs side instead set off for Africa where they played in Nigeria and Ghana. Hibs met a Ghana select side and, somewhat ignominiously, lost the match 1-0. The tour also included a draw against the Nigerian Olympic side and a victory over North Ghana.

TUESDAY 3rd JUNE 1924

Hibs European tour of Austria had a boost when they defeated Rapid Vienna 3-1 in a friendly. The Hibs manager Maley selected a strong team with many of the Cup Final team of the season just ended. Hibs took the lead in the tenth minute through Jimmy Dunn, and Harry Ritchie added a second before half-time. Ferdinand Wesely pulled a goal back for the hosts, before Harry Ritchie added his second and Hibernian's third with twelve minutes to go.

MONDAY 4th JUNE 1990

Hearts supremo Wallace Mercer announced his bid to take over city rivals Hibernian, amid the Hibees' financial problems. Mercer claimed that Edinburgh couldn't support two clubs with such small fan-bases and therefore couldn't challenge the Old-Firm. He was wrong, and his bid was met with hostility both from Hibs fans and from the vast majority of Hearts fans too. Ultimately, his bid failed and made him one of the most despised men in Edinburgh.

FRIDAY 5th JUNE 2015

Easter Road was the venue as an impressive crowd of 14,270 turned out to see Gordon Strachan's improving Scotland side take on the 2022 World Cup host Qatar. A tight game, marred with numerous substitutions as these friendly games are, was won by Scotland with a single goal from Matt Ritchie before half time. Returning to their old stomping ground

were Scotland captain Scott Brown, and second-half substitute Leigh Griffiths, who were both given a warm welcome. Former Hibees Steven Whittaker and Stephen Fletcher were unused subs.

SATURDAY 6th JUNE 1942

Hibs proved victorious in their Summer Cup encounter at Shawfield over Clyde, but it was noted that their play was 'far from satisfactory'. The game was a hard fought contest, and it was only when Clyde were reduced to ten men through injury that Hibs began to get on top in the match. After a goal-less first-half Hibs pulled away and goals from Bobby Combe and Sammy Kean settled the match in front of an impressive war time crowd of 8,000.

SUNDAY 7th JUNE 1953

Hibernian played their opening game of the Rivadavia Corrêa Meyer tournament, at the world renowned Estadio do Maracana in Rio De Janeiro in front of 33,671 fans. The Scottish team gave a good account of themselves in the searing heat of Brazil against Vasco Da Gama, at the stadium where the 1950 World Cup Final was played. All of the Famous Five played, and an inspired performance saw Hibs draw 3-3 with Eddie Turnbull and Lawrie Reilly(2) scoring, at what was the biggest stadium in the world at that time.

MONDAY 8th JUNE 1987

James 'the minute man' Kane was born. Kane has the odd 'honour' of having only played for Hibernian once, aged 16, coming on in the last minute against Livingston in a league-match in 2004, to play both his debut and his final game for Hibs. He was later transferred to Motherwell. Hibs won the match Kane played in 3-1, goals coming from Tom McManus and a brace from Derek Riordan.

WEDNESDAY 9th JUNE 1971

Pat Stanton started for Scotland, as they faced a tricky European Championship qualifier against Denmark. The Scots had been fancied to change their fortunes and qualify for the final tournament in West Germany but went down to a disappointing defeat. Former Hibs striker Colin Stein started up front, but was unable to conjure up a goal and future Hibs manager Jocky Scott came on as a second-half sub. It finished Denmark 1 Scotland 0.

TUESDAY 10th JUNE 2014

Hibernian officially sacked manager Terry Butcher, after his disastrous spell in charge of the club. Hibs had failed to win in any of the last 13 league matches of the season, and had subsequently been sucked into the play-offs, and deservedly relegated. Few bemoaned the departure of Hibernian's worst ever manager. Hibs had been mid-table when he had taken the helm.

SUNDAY 11th JUNE 1967

Hibernian were beaten 2-1 by Wolverhampton Wanderers in 'The North American Soccer League', a summer tournament in America which featured 12 established clubs, playing with American identities. Joe Davis scored for Hibs against Wolves, who ultimately won the tournament, beating Aberdeen 6-5 AET in the Final. Winners Wolves played as Los Angeles Wolves, while Hibs assumed the identity of Toronto City. Beaten finalists Aberdeen had played as Washington Whips. The whole tournament was an attempt to popularise REAL football in North America.

WEDNESDAY 12th JUNE 1990

Millionaire Tom Farmer came to the rescue of beleaguered Hibs today by buying a 'substantial number' of Hibs shares in an attempt to block Hearts Chairman Wallace Mercer's unpopular takeover bid. Mr Farmer was keen to stress that this was a blocking move with the sole intent of saving Hibs, rather than an attempt to take over the club himself.

SATURDAY 13th JUNE 1942

Hibs recorded a fine victory over Third Lanark in the Summer Cup, by eight goals to two. The forwards kept up sustained intensive pressure which was to see them suitably rewarded for their efforts. Matt Busby, guesting for the Edinburgh club during the war, was outstanding at half-back alongside Sammy Kean. Hibs goals came from Bobby Baxter, Sammy Kean, Willie Finnigan, Arthur Milne, Bobby Combe and Gordon Smith with a double, one from the penalty spot.

FRIDAY 14th JUNE 1974

Hibs' John Blackley played for Scotland in their 2-0 win over African side Zaire in the 1974 World Cup in West Germany, one of his seven caps. That Scotland team, managed by Hibs legend Willie Ormond, became the first side to ever be eliminated from the tournament on goal-difference, having beaten Zaire and drawn with Brazil and Yugoslavia in the group-stages.

SATURDAY 15th JUNE 1946

Hibs lost the Victory Cup Final to Rangers after a poor show at Hampden. Apart from a 20-minute spell towards the end of the first-half, Hibs struggled to assert their authority and former Hibby guest Jimmy Caskie helped Rangers dominate the game. Hibs' woes were attributed to Sammy Kean missing out through injury, and rather than provide a straight replacement the manager McCartney chose to make three positional changes to accommodate for his absence. This was viewed as a mistake in hindsight. Johnny Aitkenhead had equalised for Hibs late in the first-half, only for the defence to lose concentration and concede immediately afterwards. In front of 90,000 at Hampden Hibs lost 3-1.

THURSDAY 16th JUNE 1966

Another Canadian tour saw Bob Shankly's Hibs team annihilate Canadian side British Columbia All-Stars in a friendly, winning 9-2. Hibernian played six other top Canadian teams during this tour, winning every game. In the seven matches, Hibs scored 64 goals and conceded just four!

TUESDAY 17th JUNE 1947

On tour in Sweden, Hibs went down to a surprise 3-1 defeat against Norrkoping. Norrkoping featured a young Gunnar Nordahl who would later make his name in the Italian leagues. Eddie Turnbull played in this game, and recalled the local referee as one of the most biased he ever faced – three penalties were given against the Scotsmen. Turnbull was to extract an element of revenge thirty years later when the sides met in the UEFA Cup, Hibs knocking the Swedes out.

SUNDAY 18th JUNE 1967

Chicago Mustangs lost 2-1 to Toronto City in the 1967 North American Soccer League tournament. Toronto City's goals came from Peter Cormack and substitute Colin Grant, Peter Cormack was later sent-off. Chicago Mustangs were really Italian cracks Cagliari, while Toronto City were really, of course, Hibernian FC 'in disguise', as it were.

SATURDAY 19th JUNE 1943

Hibs defeated Queens Park at Easter Road in this Summer Cup second-round, second-leg tie at Easter Road. Willie McCartney's side fully merited their victory by 4-0 and the goalscorers for Hibs were Sammy Kean, Gordon Smith, Stan Williams and Charles McGillvray. Alex Hall started this game, he had been left-back of the Sunderland team that won the FA Cup in 1937, and was a regular starter for Hibs through the war, playing nearly 250 games.

FRIDAY 20th JUNE 1980

Hibs signed 17-year old striker Alan Irvine from Blackburn United. His time at Easter Road was unremarkable and he was released after two years to go to Whitburn Juniors. Irvine's career flourished thereafter and he moved on to Falkirk before being signed by Kenny Dalglish at Liverpool and Jim McLean at Dundee United. He failed to shine at both and moved onto Shrewsbury Town soon after.

SATURDAY 21st JUNE 1941

Fully 6,000 were present at Easter Road for this Summer Cup clash between Hibernian and Clyde, and it was to be the visitors who prevailed by two goals to one. Hibs had taken a second minute lead through dependable forward Arthur Milne, but Clyde came storming back to equalise before half-time, and scoring what proved to be the winning goal early in the second half. Hibs pressed in the later stages but were unable to score an equalising goal.

WEDNESDAY 22nd JUNE 1966

Hibs emulated their record victory of 15-1 over Peebles Rovers in 1961 by hammering luckless Canadian side Concordia All-Stars by the same scoreline during the club's all conquering tour of Canada.

The win over Peebles remains Hibs' 'official' record competitive win, though the Hibees did beat the 42nd Highland Regiment AKA The Black Watch 22-1 in the Scottish Cup third round, back in 1881, just before the regiment was sent to fight in a colonial war in Egypt.

WEDNESDAY 23rd JUNE 2004

Mark Venus and Simon Brown become the first signings of the Tony Mowbray era at Hibs. Venus was engaged as assistant manager, whilst Brown was signed as goalkeeper after the departures of Nick Colgan and Daniel Andersson. Venus also registered as a player, but only played a single game for Hibs, against Albion Rovers at New Douglas Park in a League Cup tie. Brown was to collect a winner's medal as reserve goalkeeper in the CIS Cup winning side of 2007 – he had by then lost his place in the team to youngster Andy McNeil.

THURSDAY 24th JUNE 1886

Hearts regained the Rosebery Charity Cup after a gap of two years, beating Hibs at the third attempt after two games had failed to provide an outcome. An excitable but well behaved crowd of around 4,000 fans watched the drama unfold at Powderhall. The season had taken its toll on Hibs, and whilst they matched Hearts in the contest, they weren't performing to the high levels of previous months. McKay scored a first-half goal for Hearts, and although Hibs enjoyed considerable pressure early in the second-half, they couldn't find a goal and lost 1-0.

SUNDAY 25th JUNE 1967

Hibernian were playing as Toronto City once more in the 'North American Soccer League', taking on Sunderland, who were playing in the guise of Vancouver Royal Canadians. Bob Shankly's men earned a hard-fought 2-2 draw against the Black Cats, the Hibees' goals coming from Joe Davis and Colin Stein.

SATURDAY 26th JUNE 1943

Hibs took the lead in the Summer Cup semi-final, but a solid performance by Rangers saw the Ibrox side run out victors. The two sides had faced each other in the previous two finals and this match was a tight affair right up until the last five minutes, when Rangers rounded off the scoring to win 3-1. Bobby Baxter had given Hibs the lead in the opening quarter of an hour direct from a free kick, after Gordon Smith had been fouled just outside the penalty box. It was end-to-end after that, but it was Rangers who equalised and then took the lead themselves shortly before half- time. Hibs pressed hard in the opening stages of the second half, but were unable to make a breakthrough despite the best efforts of their forwards.

MONDAY 27th JUNE 1966

Hibs beat Ottawa All-Stars by a whopping 15-0, during the club's Canadian tour. This was the second time on the tour that Bob Shankly's men had scored fifteen goals, this time, without reply!

SATURDAY 28th JUNE 1941

On a day when Rangers were held to a 5-5 draw with Hamiton Academicals, Hibs secured a draw of their own to ensure that their involvement in the Summer Cup continued at least until the replay at Ibrox the following Wednesday. Hibs had been 3-1 down at Clyde, and 5-2 down on aggregate, before a positional switch swapping Gordon Smith and Arthur Milne led to Hibs scoring three goals in eight minutes to win 4-3 on the day and finish 5-5 on aggregate. Willie Finnigan was in especially good form, scoring a hat-trick, but the outstanding performance on the pitch was by Matt Busby.

SATURDAY 29th JUNE 2013

Hibs opened up their pre-season friendlies at the Bet Butler Stadium in Dumbarton against former Hibby Ian Murray's side. A healthy crowd was in attendance barely a month after Hibs' previous game at Hampden in the Scottish Cup Final. A strong Hibs team took the lead through a well worked goal from Alex Harris, but were pegged back a few minutes later when Ally McKerracher equalised. The match provided a first sight for Hibs fans of new signings Liam Craig and Owain Tudur-Jones, who both gave a good account of themselves. Few present suspected that Hibs would be back there on league business barely a year later.

SATURDAY 30th JUNE 1945

The war years were coming to an end as Hibs contested the Summer Cup Final at Hampden against Partick Thistle. A poor game was to ensue, "Never in the history of football conflict has so little been accomplished by so many" opined the *Sunday Post* in a topical match report. Sammy Kean was absent, and Willie Finnigan missed out through injury and this hampered the Hibs forward line who were unable to find a way through the Partick Thistle defence. Hibs' opponents had opened the scoring midway through the first-half through Johnson, and whilst Hibs pushed for an equaliser, their efforts fell short and when Johnson added his second with five minutes to play there was no way back for Hibs.

HIBERNIAN FC
On This Day

JULY

SATURDAY 1st JULY 1967

Stoke City, under their most successful manager ever, Tony Waddington, beat Hibernian 2-0 in the North American Soccer League tournament. As per the tournament's bizarre format, Hibs were again 'Toronto City', while The Potters played as 'Cleveland Stokers'. Here are the names of the 12 teams who participated, along with the American 'aliases' they assumed for the duration. Hibs were, of course, Toronto City.

Boston Rovers - Shamrock Rovers (Dublin)
Chicago Mustangs -Cagliari (Italy)
Cleveland Stokers - Stoke City (England)
Dallas Tornado - Dundee United (Scotland)
Detroit Cougars - Glentoran (Northern Ireland)
Houston Stars - Bangu (Brazil)
Los Angeles Wolves - Wolverhampton Wanderers (England)
New York Skyliners - Cerro (Uruguay)
San Francisco Golden Gate Gales - ADO Den Haag (Netherlands)
Vancouver Royal Canadians - Sunderland (England)
Washington Whips - Aberdeen (Scotland)

MONDAY 2nd JULY 1990

TV news showed that the campaign to repel Wallace Mercer's hostile takeover bid, which could destroy Hibs and leave Hearts as the only Premier League side in the capital, had continued the previous evening with a rally in the Usher Hall attended by 2,000 football enthusiasts. Hearts' leading goal-scorer and self-confessed Hibs fan John Robertson attended the rally and afterwards he said: "I am here on behalf of the Hearts players who are determined as anyone else that the Hibs should survive."

SUNDAY 2nd JULY 2006

Hibernian were in Intertoto Cup action against Latvian side Dinaburg at Easter Road in the tournament's second round, first leg. Tony Mowbray's men were 1-0 up on the Latvians at half-time thanks to a Chris Killen goal, then blitzed their opponents with four goals in the second half to win the game 5-0, goals coming from Scott Brown, Ivan Sproule, David Murphy and Steven Fletcher, giving the Cabbage an almost unassailable lead to take to the Baltic.

VETRA FANS AT EASTER ROAD FOR INTERTOTO CUP TIE

SATURDAY 3rd JULY 2004

Just over 8,000 fans were at Easter Road for new boss Tony Mowbray's first competitive home match. The opponents were FK Vetra of Lithuania in the Intertoto Cup. Heavy rain made the match a bit of a struggle for both sides. A 'stramash' in Hibs' box allowed Sasnauska to put Vetra 1-0 up after 63 minutes but that goal was cancelled out by a late Garry O'Connor strike from 16-yards. Vetra had an all important away-goal for the second leg, but in the end, that didn't really matter, as Hibs lost 1-0 in Vilnius and were eliminated 1-2 on aggregate. FK Vetra ceased to exist in 2010 after going bust.

SATURDAY 4th JULY 1942

Defending champions Hibs lost their grip on the Summer Cup after extra-time had failed to yield a result, but they did so in the cruellest way possible – on the toss of a coin. Penalty kick shoot-outs may be considered an unsatisfactory solution to draws, but surely are better than what went on before. Rangers had been fortunate win, as Hibs had been handicapped by an injury to Arthur Milne inside the first five minutes. In the era before substitutes this meant Milne soldiered on immobile, but of little use to the rest of his team-mates. Matt Busby and Sammy Kean however were in superb form and the ten men gave as good as they got and only the crossbar prevented Shaw from scoring a decisive goal. Corner- kicks were used as the tie- break when the scores were level, but these were tied too, hence the ref choosing the dreaded coin to settle the match.

SATURDAY 5th JULY 1969

The Rolling Stones played a free concert in London's Hyde Park, Rod Laver beat John Newcombe in the 83rd Men's Wimbledon Final and Michael O'Neill was born in Portadown. The Northern Irishman had come to prominence as a teenager playing with Coleraine and his performances there earned him a move to Newcastle United. From there he moved on to Dundee United from where Hibs signed him in 1993. He played 112 times for Hibs, scoring 24 goals – many of them spectacular. He moved on to Coventry City as his contract was nearing its end, and later enjoyed promotion with Wigan Athletic. He ended his playing career at Ayr United, and became Brechin City manager in 2006, moving onto Shamrock Rovers in 2009. He was appointed Northern Ireland manager in 2011.

SUNDAY 6th JULY 2008

It was Intertoto Cup time for The Hibees again, as Mixu Paatelainen's men took on Swedish side Elfsborg in the second round, 1st leg at Easter Road. Hibs lost 2-0 in front of just over 8,000 fans, the Swedes scoring a goal in each half. The scoreline was repeated in the second leg in Boras, meaning that Hibernian went out 0-4 on aggregate.

SATURDAY 7th JULY 1951

At the 58th Wimbledon, Doris Hart beat Shirley Fry in the Ladies Final, and Malky Robertson was born. Malky came to Hibs late in his career after a chance meeting with the then Hibs manager Pat Stanton, who offered him a short term contract. Malky had previously played with Hearts, but had left them for Toronto Blizzard and it was from Dundee United he arrived where he had been on another short-term contract. He wasn't kept on after his initial trial period and played just five games for Hibs, although curiously he was unbeaten as a Hibs player and all his matches were at Easter Road. He left Edinburgh and moved onto Hamrun Spartans. His son Sandy was also a footballer, and had noted spells at Rangers, Dundee United and Inverness Caledonian Thistle and was a Scottish under 21 cap.

SATURDAY 8th JULY 2006

A pathetically small crowd of just 350, which included 120 Hibbies, watched the second leg of Hibs V Dinaburg in Daugavpils, which the Hibees won, a brace from Amadou Konte 'The Mali Magician' and a goal from Ivan Sproule giving Hibs a 3-0 win to take Hibs through 8-0 on aggregate. Dinaburg have since ceased to exist as a club, having folded in 2007 amid accusations of corruption and match-fixing.

THURSDAY 9th JULY 1987

A pre-season friendly in Verl, West Germany, saw Alex Miller's Hibees trounce the regimental football team of The Royal Scots, Hibs winning 9-0. At the time, large numbers of British troops were stationed in West Germany, as The Cold War still hung over Europe, though it was beginning to thaw.

TUESDAY 10th JULY 2007

John Collins took his Hibernian side up to Glebe Park, to play Brechin City in a pre-season friendly. Former Hibs legend Michael O'Neill was Brechin's manager and his team matched the Hibees well, only going down to a couple of late goals from Abdessalam Benjelloun and Clayton Donaldson. Brechin City 0 Hibs 2.

SATURDAY 11th JULY 1987

Continuing their tour of West Germany, Alex Miller's Hibs side took on SC Preusen in the Preusenstadion. The German minnows were no match for Hibernian, who ran out easy 4-1 winners.

SATURDAY 12th JULY 1941

In front of 37,000 at Hampden, Willie McCartney's young Hibs side became the first winners of the wartime Summer Cup. Hibs weren't fancied before this match, and there weren't many people inside the ground who gave Hibs a chance as they fell two goals behind in the opening 20-minutes. This Hibs side was made of sterner stuff though, and guided by the promptings of the veteran Matt Busby they slowly but surely fought their way into the match. They reduced the deficit from the penalty-spot, Willie Finnigan scoring after Arthur Milne had been brought down, and then the same player levelled the match just after the hour mark. Hibs were rampant now, and should have had at least two more penalties but the referee mysteriously failed to award them. Rangers still had their chances though, and James Kerr in the Hibs goal was mightily relieved to see shots rebound off the post and bar when he was beaten. It was to fall to Bobby Baxter to settle the tie in the 88th minute and Hibs lifted the cup 3-2.

TUESDAY 13th JULY 1999

Ian Murray at 18 years old achieved a lifetime ambition and signed for his boyhood heroes. A product of the Dundee United youth set up, he quickly settled into Easter Road and he made his debut the following season at Tannadice in a 0-0 draw. He became a regular under Alex McLeish, and played in the Scottish Cup Final of 2001. He missed the 2004 CIS Final through injury and left on a free transfer to Rangers in 2005. A subsequent move to Norwich City didn't work out and he returned to Hibs in 2008. Between both spells, Ian played 296 games for Hibs, scoring 17 goals and being rewarded with a testimonial match in 2011. He left Hibs for a second time in 2012, and the following season became manager of Dumbarton, where he oversaw a remarkable transformation from relegation certainties to mid-table safety. He was to remain there for the following two seasons, becoming St Mirren manager in 2015.

SATURDAY 14th JULY 2001

Alex Mcleish's men were in France to play a friendly against Marseille, one of Franck Sauzee's old clubs, where the big Frenchman had been part of the team which had won the very first Champions League tournament in season 1992-93. It was Bastille Day, and the kicking-match that ensued, while not as violent as the Bastille's storming in 1789, was certainly as passionate. Goals from Alen Orman and Garry O'Connor gave Hibernian a 2-1 win over the French giants, whose consolation strike came courtesy of a Grant Brebner own-goal. The crowd at this friendly was 2,500.

FRIDAY 15th JULY 1983

Pat Stanton took his Hibs side up to the Isle of Lewis to play a friendly match against a Stornoway XI. The plucky islanders gave the Hibees no real problems, the men from Leith winning comfortably, 4-0.

THURSDAY 16th JULY 1992

Gayfield Park in Arbroath was the venue as Alex Miller's men warmed up for the coming season with a friendly against Mickey Lawson's Red Lichties. The Hibees won the match 3-0.

WEDNESDAY 17th JULY 1940

Hibernian legend Joe Baker was born, to Scottish parents, in Liverpool. He scored an astonishing 158 goals in 194 appearances during his two spells at Hibs, 1957-1961 and 1971-1972. He also played for Torino, Arsenal, Nottingham Forest, Sunderland and Raith Rovers, finishing his playing career at the latter after his second spell at Easter Road. He also played for England, as the rules of the day dictated that he had to play for the country that he was born in. He made eight appearances for England, scoring three times. As to his time at Hibs, he scored all four goals in the Hibees'

4-3 win over Hearts in the Scottish Cup in 1958 when he was just 17 years old, he once scored nine goals in one game, in the famous 15-1 rout of Peebles Rovers in 1961, and Baker still holds the club record for league goals scored in one season, scoring 42 goals in 33 league games in season 1959-60. He was a true Hibernian great.

TUESDAY 18th JULY 2000

FSV Mainz were the opposition as Alex McLeish's men began what would become a five-match unbeaten pre-season tour of Germany. In the carnival city's Stadion am Bruchweg, the two sides huffed and puffed their way to a 0-0 draw, in sweltering heat.

SATURDAY 19th JULY 1997

Having just avoided relegation the previous season, Jim Duffy took his new-look Hibs side to Lurgan to play Glenavon, as part of Hibernian's pre-season tour of Northern Ireland. The Irishmen were no match for Jim Duffy's side, who triumphed 6-0! Striker Greg Miller, son of former Hibs boss Alex, scored a hat-trick, John Hughes scored a header and Tony Rougier bagged two late, stunning strikes.

SATURDAY 20th JULY 2002

Bobby Williamson took Hibs on a pre-season tour of Finland. This game saw the Hibees take on Tervarit in the city of Oulu. Hibs fielded a strong side, with midfielder Freddy Aprinon pulling the strings and scoring a delicious 25-yard effort after 16 minutes, to add to Paco Luna's fourth minute opener. It finished 2-0 to Hibernian, much to the delight of the 98 Hibbies in Tervarit's tiny stadium.

FRIDAY 21st JULY 1972

Tolka Park stadium in Dublin saw Eddie Turnbull's men take on the Irishmen of Home Farm, in a tedious 0-0 draw as part of Hibernian's tour of Ireland. Home Farm are best known as the club where Nicky Byrne began his playing career in the early 90's , a career which he later abandoned in favour of joining pop-group Westlife, but he later coached the Dublin side from 2008-10. Westlife often went to watch Hibs play whenever they were in Scotland doing a gig in the early noughties.

SATURDAY 22nd JULY 1989

Alex Miller's men played a friendly against Fortuna Dusseldorf at the Rheinstadion as Hibs were back in Germany for another pre-season mini-tour. Hibs lost the match 3-2, but remained unbeaten for the remainder of the tour.

SATURDAY 22nd JULY 2006

Down 1-0 from the first leg in Denmark, Tony Mowbray's Hibs looked to overturn the narrow deficit in the second leg of their third round Intertoto Cup tie against OB Odense. It was 0-0 at half-time, then Grahn scored for Odense six minutes after the restart. Towering defender Rob Jones headed Hibs level a few minutes later and then Paul Dalglish put the Cabbage 2-1 up with ten minutes remaining, but despite a valiant effort from the men in green, Odense defended well and held on, losing 2-1 in Edinburgh but going through by the away goals rule, the tie finishing 2-2 on aggregate. Former Hibs favourite Ulrik Laursen was playing for Odense.

THURSDAY 23rd JULY 1998

Alex Mcleish's men welcomed West Ham United to Easter Road for a friendly match, a match which also saw the new north stand, built in 1995, re-Christened the 'Famous Five Stand' in memory of the Hibs legends, and also, no doubt, as a morale booster for the fans following the previous season's relegation. West Ham fielded their full strength team, but the match finished in a 1-1 draw. The game saw home debuts for Hibs' Austrian players Peter Guggi and Klaus Dietrich, both of whom would soon fade into obscurity.

THURSDAY 24th JULY 1958

Jim Leighton was born in Johnstone, Renfrewshire. He made his footballing name under Alex Ferguson at Aberdeen and then at Manchester Utd until he was dropped after a poor-performance in the 1990 FA Cup Final and began a downward spiral that saw him end up at Dundee in 1992. A 3-6 defeat to Partick Thistle in 1992 saw him dropped at Dens Park, and his career looked over, until Alex Miller signed him for Hibs in the summer of 1993, giving him another chance at his career. Leighton's confidence returned at Hibs, his form in his first season helping Hibs reach the League Cup Final.

He played for Hibs until the end of season 96-97, when he returned to play for his first club, Aberdeen, after helping Hibs avoid relegation. He played 178 games for Hibernian and, like Goram, was often the difference between Hibs losing and winning games. While at Hibs, he resurrected his international career, which ultimately led to him playing at the World Cup in France in 1998, he had also played at Mexico '86 and Italia '90. In short, his free transfer to Hibs in 1993 was good for Hibs and good for him. When he came to Hibs, he replaced the combination of Chris Reid and John Burridge, who had played alternating periods in goal for the club in season 1992-93.

FRIDAY 24th JULY 1992

Alex Miller's men drew 3-3 with Highland League side Deveronvale in the Deveronvale pre-season mini-tournament. Hibs won the resulting penalty shoot-out 5-3. Deveronvale is the club from which the Hibees signed Des Bremner in the 1970's.

MONDAY 25th JULY 1966

Darren Jackson was born in Edinburgh. Hibs signed Jackson in the summer of 1992 as both the fans and boss Alex Miller knew that Keith Wright needed a strike-partner. Hibs couldn't agree a transfer fee with his club Dundee Utd, so the fee was decided by a transfer tribunal, as it was the pre-Bosman era. That fee was £400,000. He scored on his debut for Hibs in a friendly against Blackburn Rovers, but had to wait until early September for his first competitive strike, against his old club Dundee Utd in a 2-1 win at Easter Road. Jackson was initially a striker and was often booked for mouthing off at referees, but he, and Alex Miller, worked together to make him into more of an attacking midfielder, this, combined with his weight-training, helped transform him into a brilliant, strong, solid player, who it could be argued carried Hibs on the park for much of the mid 90's. His improvement at Hibs got him a Scotland call-up. He was sold to Celtic in the summer of 1997, and Hibs simply couldn't replace him. He scored 59 goals in 206 appearances for Hibs, a quarter of them penalties, many more of them decisive strikes in important matches.

HIBS IN ACTION AGAINST SUNDERLAND IN 2003

THURSDAY 25th JULY 2013

Down 0-2 from the first leg in Sweden,, Hibs faced Malmo at Easter Road in the second leg of their Europa League tie. Pat Fenlon's men were utterly annihilated by the Swedes, going in at half-time 0-4 down, and conceding three more goals in the second half to lose 0-7 on the night, 0-9 on aggregate. The only highlights for Hibs fans on that sunny evening were moving renditions of 'Sunshine On Leith' and 'Hail Hail' before kick-off, in tribute to legend Lawrie Reilly, who had died a few days before the game.

SATURDAY 26th JULY 2003

Bobby Williamson's men warmed up for the new season by hosting English first division side Sunderland at Easter Road in a friendly. Mick McCarthy's men led 1-0 at half-time thanks to a Kevin Kyle header. New striker Stephen Dobbie came on for Hibs at the interval and made an impact, scoring two great goals to put Hibs 2-1 up. John Oster equalised for the Black Cats with just seven minutes remaining and it finished Hibs 2 Sunderland 2.

SATURDAY 27th JULY 1991

Alex Miller's men were up in the highlands playing a friendly against local side Nairn County. Hibernian did the smaller side no favours and annihilated them 9-0.

MONDAY 27th JULY 1992

Big-spending Blackburn Rovers were the visitors for a pre-season friendly at Easter Road. Rovers, who like Hibs were formed in 1875, brought up a strong side which included new British transfer record signing Alan Shearer. Hibs comfortably won the match 3-0. Back then, the English season started several weeks after Scotland's, which meant that Scottish teams were always two weeks ahead in pre-season training, and this usually showed when they played each other. Hibernian's goals came from Tommy McIntyre, Brian Hamilton and a strike on his debut for Darren Jackson.

SATURDAY 28th JULY 2001

Hibs played host to Kilmarnock, hoping for a 'Christening gift' for the newly opened West Stand, which had replaced the iconic but outdated Main Stand. As was often the case when Alex Mcleish's Hibees took on Bobby Williamson's Killie, it was a close game. Ulises De Le Cruz, Alen Orman, Paco Luna and Craig Brewster all made their debuts for the Cabbage. Michel Ngonge silenced Easter Road in the fourth minute, putting Kilmarnock 1-0 up, but Hibs were level at the interval thanks to a Franck Sauzee penalty – or so it seemed, Christophe Cocard restoring Killie's lead with the first half's last kick. Hibs huffed and puffed, but had to wait until seven minutes from the end for an equaliser, Ulrik Laursen bundling the ball home after an error from Kilmarnock 'keeper Gordon Marshall. In the end, the 2-2 draw was a fair result.

MONDAY 29th JULY 2002

Davie Moyes' Everton visited Easter Road for a pre-season friendly, bringing a strong team north. Pre-match hype had been centred around Everton's new 'wonder-kid', 16-year-old Wayne Rooney, and he soon made his mark, giving the Toffees the lead with a header after 30 minutes. Garry O'Connor gave Alan Stubbs the slip to equalise after 37 minutes, then Tam McManus gave the Hibees the lead after 50 minutes, his goal celebration showing his delight at scoring against such a top side. Everton were no mugs though, and pressed Hibs hard, finally equalising four minutes from time with a David Unsworth penalty, awarded after a silly handball by Matt Doumbe. It finished 2-2.

WEDNESDAY 30th JULY 1975

Hibs concluded their successful tour of Ireland by beating Ireland's oldest club, Bohemians, 1-0 at Dublin's Dalymount Park. During the tour, Eddie Turnbull's men had also thrashed Waterford Utd 6-0 and beaten Cork Hibernians, now Cork City, 2-0.

WEDNESDAY 31st JULY 1974

There were 28,000 fans at Easter Road to see a thrilling Drybrough Cup semi- final between Hibs and Rangers. A double from Joe Harper wasn't enough for the Cabbage, who lost 3-2, Rangers' goals coming from MacDonald, Parlane and Fyfe. On this occasion, Hibbies sang "all we are saying, is give us a goal" to a famous John Lennon tune, as many fans did back then.

SATURDAY 31st JULY 1999

Newly promoted Hibs welcomed big-spending Motherwell to Easter Road for the season opener. A superb atmosphere ensued, with the chorus 'Hibees are back' reverberating around the stadium. A decent performance saw Hibs draw 2-2 with the Steelmen, both of Hibs' goals coming from new German striker Dirk Lehmann. Hibs were back where they belonged, in the big-time!

HIBERNIAN FC
On This Day

AUGUST

WEDNESDAY 1st AUGUST 1979

Hibs lost 0-1 at Easter Road to St Mirren in the second leg of the two teams' preliminary tie in the Anglo-Scottish Cup. The Paisley side edged out Eddie Turnbull's men 4-3 on aggregate, the first leg at Love Street having ended 3-3. Hibernian's goals in the first leg were scored by George Stewart, Jim Brown and Tony Higgins. The Buddies went on to win the tournament, the only Scottish side to do so. The Anglo-Scottish Cup was a summer tournament which had replaced the Texaco Cup. The Texaco Cup was contested by teams from Scotland, England, Ireland and Northern Ireland, but the Anglo-Scottish Cup was contested, as the name suggests, just by Scots and English ones.

WEDNESDAY 2nd AUGUST 1972

Over 27,000 fans at Easter Road saw Hibernian defeat Rangers 3-0 in the Drybrough Cup semi-final. It was the 'Gers first match since they had won the 1972 Cup Winners Cup Final. The Hibees' goals came from Pat Stanton and a brace from Alan Gordon.

SUNDAY 3rd AUGUST 1997

Jim Duffy's new-look side started the season in style, beating Celtic 2-1 at Easter Road. Lee Power gave Hibs a first half lead, but Malky Mackay equalised for the Hoops a few minutes later. A misplaced pass by new signing Henrik Larsson allowed Hibs' Chic Charnley to score a deserved winner for Duffy's men in the second half, and many Hibs fans looked forward to a good season. In contrast, many Celtic fans were unhappy with the new signing Larsson, who had disappointed them.

SATURDAY 3rd AUGUST 2002

Hibs opened the season at home to Aberdeen, and took the lead through Francisco Javier Aguilera in the first half. However, it wasn't to be an opening day win for Bobby Williamson's men, as Darren Mackie equalised for the Dons on the hour, then Chris Clark scored a late, somewhat undeserved winner for Aberdeen SEVEN minutes into injury time.

SATURDAY 4th AUGUST 1973

In the sun at Hampden 50,000 fans saw Eddie Turnbull's men beat Celtic 1-0 to win the Drybrough Cup. The match was goal-less after 90 minutes, the extra-time winner coming in the 119th minute, courtesy of an Alan Gordon strike from 17 yards.

TUESDAY 4th AUGUST 1998

Relegated Hibs kicked off their division one campaign at the not-so glamorous venue of Cappielow, against Morton. Hibs won the match 1-0 thanks to a goal from Barry Lavety. It wasn't exactly 'total football', but it was a good start. Stuart Lovell and Paul Holsgrove made their Hibernian debuts in this game.

SATURDAY 5th AUGUST 1972

Hibs took on Celtic in the Drybrough Cup Final at Hampden in front of nearly 50,000 fans. The Cabbage were cruising 3-0 up, thanks to a double from Alan Gordon and an own-goal by Celtic's Billy McNeil. The match was then interrupted by a pitch-invasion from Celtic fans, after which, Celtic's team gained the initiative to fight back and level the game at 3-3, with a double from Jimmy Johnstone and a goal from McNeil – at the right end this time. The match went into extra-time, the Hibees coming out on top thanks to extra-time goals from Arthur Duncan and substitute Jimmy O'Rourke. It finished Hibs 5 Celtic 3 AET.

TUESDAY 5th AUGUST 1986

A glamour pre-season friendly saw Chelsea come up to play John Blackley's Hibs at Easter Road, as part of the 'deal' that saw striker Gordon Durie move to the London side. Hibs tore Chelsea apart, with a hat-trick from Willie Irvine, who had been signed from Stirling Albion for a mere £30,000, and a second half strike from Paul Kane. Chelsea's late consolation goal was scored by big Joe McLaughlin, who later ended up playing for Hibs in the mid 90's.

FRIDAY/SUNDAY 6th AUGUST 1875

A meeting held in the Catholic Institute in St Mary's Street led to the formation of Hibernian Football Club. The unlikely pair of gentlemen behind the move were Canon Edward Hannan and

Michael Whelehan, both men born in Ireland and later having moved to Edinburgh. Michael, along with his friends, had taken an interest in playing and watching football, which had become common at The Meadows and at other places in Edinburgh. Other clubs were reluctant to include Irish players, so they formed their own club and despite initial hostility became an accepted part of the Edinburgh football scene. Hibs' centenary captain, Pat Stanton, is a direct descendant of Michael Whelehan.

SUNDAY 7th AUGUST 1994

Premiership giants Sheffield Wednesday visited Easter Road for a friendly, a decent-sized away support occupying the now-seated but still uncovered Dunbar end, while the East Terrace re-opened as the 'East Stand', sporting a reduced capacity because it was now seated. Throughout the match, Hibbies, who were unused to sitting at games, began the habit of getting up and down so that they could see goalmouth incidents, yet the singing never stopped. The match itself was thrilling. Hibs defeated Trevor Francis' Owls 3-2, Hibs' goals coming from an early Darren Jackson penalty, Stephen Tweed, and a late winner from Gareth Evans. Ian Taylor and Mark Bright netted for 'Wednesday.

SATURDAY 7th AUGUST 2004

Tony Mowbray's first home league game in charge saw Hibs take on Kilmarnock on the season's opening day. It wasn't quite the start Hibernian wanted – Killie winning the match 1-0 thanks to a late strike by Kris Boyd.

SATURDAY 8th AUGUST 1999

A Sunday evening kick-off for SKY saw Hibs travel to Dens Park to play Dundee. In a game which was a great advert for Scottish football, Dirk Lehman gave Hibs an early lead, but Dundee hit back, going 2-1 up after the break, before Franck Sauzee equalised for Hibs with a trademark free-kick. Dundee then went 3-2 up via an Eddie Annand penalty, before Franck Sauzee scored again, this time volleying a Latapy corner past Rab Douglas to make it 3-3. Young Kenny Miller produced a moment of brilliance in the last minute, controlling a Paul Lovering throw-in then turning to curl a wonderful shot into the net, to give the Hibees a 4-3 victory.

SATURDAY 9th AUGUST 1986

Rangers' new expensively assembled squad under new player-manager Graeme Souness faced an opening day trip to Easter Road. The home side won the match 2-1 with goals from Stuart Beedie and Steve Cowan, Ally McCoist netting the 'Gers goal from the penalty spot, but the result was overshadowed by extraordinary events that occurred on the pitch in between play. Souness was sent off for a disgusting, very deliberate tackle on Hibs' George McCluskey which broke the veteran forward's leg. As a result of that challenge, a mass brawl between the opposing teams took place on the pitch, with every single player being booked apart from Hibs' 'keeper Alan Rough, who was the only player who avoided the 'stramash' and thus received no yellow card.

SATURDAY 9th AUGUST 1997

Hibs defeated Alloa Athletic 3-1 at Easter Road in the League Cup. Goals came from Barry Lavety, Pat McGinlay and Chic Charnley. The latter's goal was a stunning opportunistic effort from inside the Hibs half! Sadly for those not in attendance, and for posterity, there were no cameras present at the game, so no video footage of that wonder-goal exists.

SATURDAY 9th AUGUST 2014

Relegated Hibs, under new manager Alan Stubbs, kicked of their Championship campaign for promotion by beating Livingston 2-1 at Easter Road. Farid El Alagui gave Hibs the lead after 16 minutes, then, after 20 minutes, Hibernian 'keeper Mark Oxley scored directly from a clearance from his own box, much to the shame of Livi goalie Darren Jamieson, who mis-judged the kick in much the same way that David Wylie had when Andy Goram had scored for Hibs from a clearance, shooting the other way, back in 1988. Gallagher scored Livingston's consolation goal.

SATURDAY 10th AUGUST 1946

Hibs opened up their first season of peacetime football since 1939 with a resounding victory over Queen of the South. Jock Cuthbertson opened the scoring in the first minute and the Edinburgh side dominated the Dumfries visitors, finishing up 9-1 victors in front of a booming post-war crowd of 30,000. Gordon Smith was unstoppable, creating many of the goals, and even more chances that weren't taken. Jock Weir scored four and Jock Cuthbertson got two. Johnny Aitkenhead, Archie Buchanan and Smith himself were the other Hibs goalscorers. An interesting postscript to this game: it was the first occasion that Hibs wore numbered jerseys.

SUNDAY 11th AUGUST 2002

The first Edinburgh derby of the season at Tynecastle saw Jambos' Dutch striker Mark De Vries score four of Hearts' five goals in their 5-1 victory over the Easter Road men. Andy Kirk had opened the scoring in the first half, while Ian Murray had netted what turned out to be Hibs' consolation goal just after the break. The scoreline flattered Hearts as it came about thanks to a late defensive collapse from Hibs and bad goalkeeping by Tony Caig, but the Jambos deserved their victory nonetheless.

SATURDAY 11th AUGUST 2007

SPL new-boys Gretna visited Easter Road for the first league meeting between the sides. Fabian Yantorno's free-kick gave Gretna a half-time lead, which they doubled just after the interval. Benji then had a penalty saved, but his fellow Moroccan Merouane Zemmama scored after 64 minutes, then Steven Fletcher equalised for Hibs two minutes later. A half-time 'roasting' from John Collins had made Hibs step up a gear and Gretna had no answer to the onslaught. Zemmama scored again with eight minutes left and a Kevin McCann strike in the last minute gave Hibs a 4-2 win, but it should've been more. Hibs never lost a match to Gretna during their brief, doomed spell in senior Scottish football. Gretna's tiny support at the game was teased by Hibs fans in the East Stand singing 'three fans, you've only got three fans!'.

SATURDAY 12th AUGUST 2000

Alex Mcleish's Hibs side played host to Dundee on a hot sunny Saturday in the SPL. This time, Dundee's team was full of foreign stars brought in by new boss Ivano Bonetti. Hibs' excellent start to the season looked under-threat when Fabian Caballero put Dundee 1-0 up after just seven minutes, but the Hibees came storming back. Eight minutes later, short-term signing Didier Agathe equalised for

Hibs with a stunning solo effort, before scoring his and Hibs' second after 40 minutes. Dirk Lehmann scored two goals in two minutes in the 82nd and 83rd, and Stuart Lovell completed the rout five minutes from full-time. Dundee had two players sent off in this game (one at full time), and Russell Latapy also missed a penalty in the first half.

SATURDAY 13th AUGUST 1994

Hibs' season got off to a perfect start at Easter Road as Alex Miller's rampant side utterly annihilated Dundee Utd. Hibs won 5-0, with goals from Billy Findlay, Michael O'Neill, two from Darren Jackson, who seemed to love scoring against his former club, and a goal from substitute Kevin Harper. Dundee Utd were relegated that season.

SATURDAY 14th AUGUST 1999

After a season with no derby due to Hibs' spell in division one, the fixture was back. Hibs took the lead through a first half Russell Latapy penalty, but Gary McSwegan equalised for Hearts in the second half. It finished 1-1. This game is best remembered for a humorous incident involving Hearts midfielder Steve Fulton. Constantly goaded by the Hibs fans about his striking features, Fulton was being given a talking to by the referee for a foul, when another verbal tirade was launched at him from the East Stand. Fulton reacted to the tirade by gesturing to the Hibs fans, so the referee booked him. The chants from the terracing changed to 'booked for being ugly, you've just been booked for being ugly', much to the mirth of all in attendance.

SATURDAY 15th AUGUST 2009

John Hughes' men took on St Mirren at home in the league. It was a memorable debut for young David Wotherspoon, who scored for Hibs on his first outing just before half-time, to cancel out Stephen McGinn's opener within a minute of the Buddies scoring. Gus Macpherson's side had been reduced to ten-men after 15 minutes, striker Steven Thompson getting a straight red for a disgusting challenge on Hibs' Patrick Cregg. Abdessalam 'Benji' Benjelloun's first Hibernian goal in almost two years proved the winner, the striker coming on as a substitute to score with a diving-header in the 83rd minute to make it Hibs 2 St Mirren 1.

SATURDAY 16th AUGUST 1902

Hibs opened up was to be their first Scottish Division One title winning season with a hard fought home draw against Celtic. A healthy crowd of 7,000 turned up to see a rematch of the Scottish Cup Final which Hibernian had won at Parkhead in April. Celtic managed to exert considerable pressure and scored the opening goal through Campbell in the first half. Hibs performed better after that, but at half-time it was the visitors who held the lead. Hibs were much better after the break and although it looked like McPherson in the Celtic goal might keep a clean sheet, Hibs finally equalised from the penalty spot through Archie Gray. Hibs were to win the return fixture at Parkhead in January, 4-0.

WEDNESDAY 17th AUGUST 1988

Substitute Steve Archibald made an impact on his debut, netting twice as Alex Miller's men bulldozed Stranraer 4-0 in round two of the League Cup. Hibs' other goals came from Paul Kane and Gareth Evans in what was an easy win. Archibald's signing had raised many an eyebrow, Hibs getting the famous former Scotland international from Barcelona in an ambitious move.

SATURDAY 17th AUGUST 2003

Bobby Williamson secured what was to be his only Edinburgh derby win as Hibernian manager, in this league match at Easter Road. Hibs played most of the match with just ten-men, as Grant Brebner was harshly red-carded in the first half. Hibs secured a 1-0 victory in the dying minutes when Garry O'Connor smashed the ball past Hearts"keeper Tepi Moilanen into the net at the home end of the ground.

SATURDAY 18th AUGUST 1962

Walter Galbraith's side took on the now defunct Third Lanark in the group stage of the League Cup. The Hibees won a thrilling match 3-2, goals coming from an own goal by Third Lanark and a double from John Fraser. The return match at Cathkin Park was won 4-1 by the Cabbage, thanks to a hat-trick from Gerry Baker and a goal from Morris Stevenson. Third Lanark ceased to exist in 1967.

SATURDAY 19th AUGUST 1989

Stunning displays by midfield maestro John Collins and 'keeper Andy Goram gave Hibs a well-deserved victory over champions Rangers at Easter Road. Second half goals from Keith Houchen and fans' favourite Mickey Weir gave Hibs the win, the latter goal coming after an almost comical mistake by Rangers' Israeli goalie Bonni Ginzburg.

SATURDAY 20th AUGUST 1960

There were 15,000 fans at Easter Road to see Hugh Shaw's men annihilate Airdrieonians in the League Cup, Hibs winning 6-1. Hibs' goals came from Joe Baker, who scored four, John Baxter and a goal from Bobby Johnstone, the last of his 142 goals for Hibernian, in what would turn out to be his penultimate game for the Hibees.

WEDNESDAY 21st AUGUST 1901

Hibs began their 1901/02 season as they would end it; with a game at Parkhead against Celtic. As the season was to end, there would be but a single goal separating the sides, but on this occasion it was Celtic who prevailed in this Glasgow Exhibition Cup first round tie in glorious weather with a bumper crowd. Celtic had scored early in the game, and despite the game ebbing and flowing most observers considered Hibs to be worthy of an equalising goal. In the latter stages, Hibs pressed incessantly, but a combination of poor finishing and desperate defending was to allow Celtic to triumph.

TUESDAY 22nd AUGUST 1989

Clydebank held Hibs for 120 minutes in this League Cup third round tie at Easter Road. Hibs beat the now defunct Bankies 5-3 on penalties, Hibs keeper Andy Goram taking, and scoring, one of the Hibees' kicks.

SATURDAY 22nd AUGUST 1992

An Edinburgh Derby at Easter Road saw Hibs squander the chance to end their long win-less run against their city rivals, which stretched back to 1989. Darren Jackson was denied his first competitive goal for Hibernian when his headed goal was ruled out for offside, later replays showing that he hadn't been, and Hibs missed many chances, the pick of which came in the first half. Hibs were awarded a penalty but Brian Hamilton's thunderbolt from the spot was brilliantly saved by Henry Smith. Despite dominating the game, Hibs were unable to score and it ended 0-0. Henry Smith, in an after-match interview, said that he had known where Hamilton would place his penalty, as he had seen a handy diagram in the match programme, showing where Hamilton had placed the penalty he had scored against Raith in the League Cup 10 days previously. After this derby, Hearts boss Joe Jordan simply said 'we were lucky'.

SATURDAY 23rd AUGUST 1997

Jim Duffy's flamboyant Hibs side thrashed Kilmarnock 4-0 at Easter Road to go top of the league. Goals from Willie Miller, Barry Lavety, Stevie Crawford and Pat McGinlay sealed the rout, the latter's goal being a long range effort from just one yard inside the Kilmarnock half, prompting a good-natured debate between McGinlay and Chic Charnley, who had scored from a similar distance against Alloa a few games previously. Asides a 5-2 win at home against Dunfermline a fortnight later, Hibs didn't win another match until January 1998, and ended up being relegated.

WEDNESDAY 24th AUGUST 1977

Hibs were humbled at home by Queen of the South in round one of the League Cup, losing the first leg of the tie 1-2, Ally MacLeod scoring Hibs' goal. The second leg at Palmerston ended goalless, Hibs thus falling at the first hurdle, losing 2-1 on aggregate.

WEDNESDAY 25th AUGUST 1965

Bob Shankly's men opened their league campaign with a trip to Cappielow to play Morton. The Hibees were too strong for the home side and ran out 5-1 winners in the end, goals coming courtesy of Peter Cormack, Pat Quinn, Jim Scott and a double from Neil Martin, in front of just under 7,000 fans. Hibs had already beaten Morton 4-2 in the League Cup at Cappielow four days earlier.

SATURDAY 26th AUGUST 1950

The weather intervened as Hibs' League Cup sectional tie at Dens Park was abandoned due to a waterlogged pitch with 23 minutes of the game remaining. Hibs had dominated the game and were two goals to the good by that point thanks to goals either side of half time from Lawrie Reilly. The change in weather was startling as in the first half the sizeable crowd had basked in sunshine, but the referee, Mr Gerrard of Aberdeen, had no option as conditions and play became farcical. Unusually for a Scottish competitive fixture, the match was never replayed. By the time the date set for the replay – 6 September – came around, Hibs had already won the section, so a decision was made to set aside the fixture.

SATURDAY 27th AUGUST 2005

Tony Mowbray left out Derek Riordan for Hibs' league visit to Ibrox, leaving many among the small visiting Hibs support a little apprehensive about the game against the big-spending Glasgow giants. Hibernian weathered the storm in the first half, Rangers squandering many scoring chances. Garry O'Connor was substituted after 63 minutes with the score still at 0-0, and seemed very angry about it, but he was replaced by Irish winger Ivan Sproule, who had been signed for the princely sum of just £5,000 from Irish side Institute the previous season, going full-time at Hibs and giving up his full-time job as a fabrication engineer. Hibs changed tactics and Sproule opened the scoring just four minutes after coming on, coolly lobbing Rangers' 'keeper Waterreus. Sproule added his and Hibs' second after 84 minutes with another sublime finish, then completed his hat-trick in injury time, giving Hibs their first win at Ibrox in ten years, to the delight of the small band of Hibs fans seated in the corner, and those listening on the radio at home. The wee engineer had 'engineered' a Hibs win that has went down in Hibs folklore, referred to simply as the 'Sproule' game. Sproule himself was a Rangers fan, but that wasn't evident in his jubilant goal celebrations.

SATURDAY 28th AUGUST 1976

The League Cup group stage saw St Johnstone visit Easter Road. Pat Stanton made his last appearance for Hibernian prior to his move to Celtic, coming on as a substitute. 5,700 fans watched Eddie Turnbull's side thrash the Saints 9-2! Hibernian's goals came from two John Brownlie penalties, a brace apiece from Ally MacLeod and Lindsay Muir and strikes from Des Bremner, Arthur Duncan and Ally Scott.

WEDNESDAY 29th AUGUST 1984

Managed by Pat Stanton, Hibs suffered a shock in round three of the League Cup at Easter Road, losing 2-1 to the now defunct Meadowbank Thistle in front of little more than 3,000 fans. Ralph Callachan netted for Hibs in this best forgotten 'derby'. Meadowbank went all the way to the semi-finals, where they lost to Rangers.

SATURDAY 30th AUGUST 1952

Hibs and Celtic faced off in the final League Cup sectional game, with Hibs holding a superior goal average and Celtic a two point lead. This meant that Hibs had to win to progress whilst a draw would be enough for Celtic, and a huge crowd of 52,000 in Leith attended in support of both teams. Hibs were still without the injured Paterson and Gallagher, and were unchanged from their previous game. The Easter Road side performed admirably and the Famous Five were at their imperious best. Eddie Turnbull put Hibs ahead, and Lawrie Reilly scored a second in the 27th minute. Hibs changed ends to shoot down the slope at half-time, and Reilly added a third in the 80th minute for Hibs to progress to the knock-out stages, where they were to lose out at the semi-final stage to Dundee.

WEDNESDAY 31st AUGUST 1988

There were 15,000 fans at Easter Road to see Alex Miller's men take on Aberdeen in the League Cup quarter-final. The Dons took the lead after ten minutes through Charlie Nicholas, but Hibs were back on level terms 15 minutes later, when Paul Kane slammed a 20-yard free-kick past Aberdeen goalie Theo Snelders. Snelders committed several fouls and was one of six players to be booked in the match, but the Dutch goalie also made some superb saves to keep Hibs at bay. Aberdeen won the match 2-1 AET, Brian Grant's goal in extra-time scraping Aberdeen through.

TUESDAY 31st AUGUST 1993

Partick Thistle hosted Hibs in the League Cup quarter-final at Firhill, and it really was a case of 'Firhill for thrills'. Roddy Grant gave the Jags the lead in the first half, only for Kevin 'Crunchie' McAllister to level things with a fine shot. Tied 1-1 at 90 minutes, the match went into extra-time. McAllister scored again to give

Hibs the edge, but Albert Craig soon equalised for Partick. 2-2 after extra-time, the match was decided by penalties. Jim Leighton was the hero and saved three penalties in the shoot-out, from Roddy Grant, Paul Kinnaird and Ian Cameron, Hibs winning 3-2 on penalties. Hibs fans who had made the trip to Maryhill for the tie sang 'Scotland's number-one' in tribute to Leighton at the end, the 'keeper having resurrected his career at Hibs under Alex Miller.

HIBERNIAN FC
On This Day

SEPTEMBER

WEDNESDAY 1st SEPTEMBER 1982

Just 1,300 fans at Broomfield saw Hibs square-off against Airdrieonians in the League Cup group stages. Bertie Auld's men lost 1-3 to the Diamonds and were eliminated from the competition, the Hibees' consolation goal coming from Gordon Rae. It was Auld's last game in charge of Hibs, he was replaced as manager by Pat Stanton. Auld had got Hibs promoted back to the Premier League in 1981 and achieved a mid-table finish in season 1981/82. He and Franck Sauzee are the only two Hibernian managers who ever won the European Champions Cup as players.

SATURDAY 2nd SEPTEMBER 1939

Willie McCartney's young side continued to be inconsistent as they fell to Albion Rovers in front of a crowd of 10,000 at Easter Road. The game would prove to have a lasting significance as it was the last peacetime game Hibs were to play for nearly six years. Hibs had rushed half-back Bobby Fraser into a return to the team, but it was clear he was not ready. Despite this, Hibs led at half-time with goals from Nutley and McLean countering an early dubious penalty for the Coatbridge team. Sammy Kean then put Hibs 3-2 ahead, but Albion equalised and in the end-to-end action that followed as Hibs sought a winner, they conceded two more to finish on the wrong end of a 5-3 scoreline.

SATURDAY 3rd SEPTEMBER 1887

Hibs opened up their defence of the Scottish Cup with a convincing first round victory at Easter Road against West Lothian side Broxburn Thistle. The game was won by half-time, and indeed all the goals were scored in the first half. George Smith opened the scoring near the half-hour mark, and soon afterwards James McGhee and Phil Clarke both scored within a minute. James McLaren scored a spectacular long rage shot, before Mick Dunbar scored a fifth to end the scoring. Hibs' cup winning side had been augmented with new additions, and the club was hopeful of continuing success in the future, following this 5-0 win.

MONDAY 4th SEPTEMBER 1961

Hugh Shaw's Hibernian took on Portuguese side Belenenses in the Fairs Cup first round first leg in front of 20,000 fans at Easter Road. The visitors stunned the home side by going in 3-0 up at half-time, but the Hibees came roaring back in the second half with two goals from John Fraser and a penalty from Sammy Baird to draw the match 3-3. 25,000 fans in Portugal saw Hibs win the second leg 3-1, thanks to a double from John Baxter and an Eric Stevenson strike, winning the tie 6-4 on aggregate. Alas, Hibs were eliminated in the next round by Red Star Belgrade 0-5 on aggregate, the damage being done in the first leg in Yugoslavia, which Hibs lost 4-0.

WEDNESDAY 4th SEPTEMBER 1985

Celtic visited Easter Road in the League Cup quarter-finals. Hibs were bottom of the league but battled hard in this thrilling tie, which finished 4-4 after extra-time, having been all square at 3-3 after normal time. Gordon Durie (2) and Steve Cowan were among Hibs' scorers. After five shots apiece in the penalty shoot-out, the teams were tied at 3-3, but the decisive kick came when Celtic's Pierce O'Leary blazed his penalty over the bar, to the jubilation of the home support. Hibs would face a two-legged semi-final against Rangers.

SATURDAY 5th SEPTEMBER 1931

Life in the lower league was not going well for Hibernian, as they lost this local derby at home to St Bernards in front of just 8,000 diehards. Bobby Templeton's side were outfoxed by their neighbours who played some attractive football to secure the victory. Hibs had taken an early lead through Paddy Burke but were pinned back, and went into half-time 3-1 down. As the match neared its conclusion Harry Brown scored to reduce the deficit to 3-2, but George Blyth the Hibernian goalkeeper gave away a late penalty, and in the incident broke his leg, and with St Bernards scoring from the resultant penalty the game finished 2-4. It wasn't the worst fate to befall a goalkeeper that day; Celtic's brilliant young goalkeeper John Thomson lost his life after an accidental collision with a Rangers player in the Old Firm derby the same day.

SATURDAY 6th SEPTEMBER 1986

Crumbling Brockville hosted this Premier League clash. A large travelling support saw Alan Irvine give the Bairns the lead, until Joe McBride equalised with a glancing header seven minutes from time, to rescue a deserved point for the Hibees.

SATURDAY 7th SEPTEMBER 1918

A miserable day at Rugby Park saw Hibs thumped by Kilmarnock 7-1. After going behind early in the game, Hibs rallied and future England International goalkeeper Harold Gough saved a penalty, before Hibs equalised through a penalty awarded at the other end which was converted by William McGinnigle. That, however, was to be as good as it got for Hibs as the goals rained in, with Kilmarnock centre Culley helping himself to a hat-trick.

WEDNESDAY 8th SEPTEMBER 1965

19,000 fans were at Easter Road for the Cabbage's first round first leg Fairs Cup tie against Spanish giants Valencia. An early headed goal by Jim Scott and a late John McNamee header gave Hibs a 2-0 win on the night. Hibs lost the second leg in Valencia by the same scoreline and as there was no extra-time back then, a toss of a coin decided where the match would be decided in a single replay. Valencia won that toss, and also won the replay in Spain 3-0.

SATURDAY 9th SEPTEMBER 1967

On league business at Easter Road, Hibs took on city-rivals Hearts in an Edinburgh derby watched by just over 20,000 fans. Hibs thumped the Jambos 4-1, largely thanks to a goal from Peter Cormack and a hat-trick from Pat Quinn, who hadn't scored for nearly two years before this game. Tommy Traynor scored for Hearts.

SATURDAY 10th SEPTEMBER 1932

Leith Athletic visited Easter Road on league business as Hibs were attempting to return to the top flight of Scottish football at the second attempt, after their abortive attempt the previous season. They had made a much better start this time around, and were convincing 3-0 winners in this local derby. The margin might have been more emphatic too had Hibs not hit the crossbar three times and eased up in the second half when the match was clearly won. Club Legend Johnny Halligan opened the scoring, and Peter McPherson added a second soon afterwards. James Hart, the centre-forward, rounded off the scoring just before half-time.

SATURDAY 11th SEPTEMBER 1886

Hibs opened up their Scottish Cup campaign at home against Durhamstown Rangers, hoping to go one better this season after losing semi-finals in previous seasons. They progressed to the next round in some style with a hat-trick from Willie Groves added to goals by George Smith and Phil Clarke. The Rangers had matched Hibs for the early part of the game, but the green jerseys ran out winners, 5-1.

SATURDAY 12th SEPTEMBER 1993

Alex Miller's men travelled to Glasgow to meet Celtic on league business, with both sides having an eye on their forthcoming UEFA Cup ties in midweek. A fine strike by Celtic's Polish full-back Darius Wdowczyk gave the 'Hoops the lead, then Keith Wright equalised just before the interval with a fine volley. Paul McStay restored Celtic's lead in the second half and it looked like a case of 'same old story' for Hibs in Glasgow. Celtic goalkeeper Gordon Marshall was one of many 'keepers struggling with the new 'pass-back' rule, and Hibs capitalised on this after 68 minutes, when Marshall made a mess of a pass-back and was dispossessed by Darren Jackson, whom he promptly hauled down, giving Hibs a rare penalty in Glasgow. Jackson took the kick himself, slamming it into the top corner to make it 2-2. The exciting match looked set to finish all square, until seven minutes from time, when Marshall foolishly charged out of his box to tackle Keith Wright, who skipped past him and squared the ball to Gareth Evans, who smashed the ball past the two Celtic defenders on the line to score the winner. Hibs won 3-2, the perfect way to prepare for the tie against Anderlecht in midweek.

WEDNESDAY 13th SEPTEMBER 1944

Pat Stanton was born in Edinburgh. Stanton is a true Hibernian legend, having played for and managed the club. His spell as manager wasn't so good as it came at a tough time in the club's history financially, but as a player, he is one of the best. He played 617 games for Hibernian and scored 78 goals from midfield in his 13 years as a player between 1963 and 1976, before joining Celtic in a straight swap for Jackie McNamara. Stanton also gained 16 Scotland caps in his career. He later made a cameo appearance as a barman in the movie adaptation of Hibs fan Irvine Welsh's novel *The Acid House*, playing 'Pat'.

THURSDAY 13th SEPTEMBER 2001

Hibs fans who had crossed Europe to see Alex Mcleish's men take on AEK Athens in the UEFA Cup found that their journey had been fruitless, not because of defeat, but because their first round first leg tie in Athens had been postponed because of the terrible terrorist attacks in New York two days before the game. Hibs lost the re-scheduled fixture in Greece 2-0, giving Alex Mcleish's men a tough task ahead in the second leg in Edinburgh.

WEDNESDAY 14th SEPTEMBER 1955

Heavy rain may have kept the crowd down to around 5,000, but Hibs opened up their European adventure in some style as they won 4-0 against Rot Weiss Essen in their inaugural European Cup game. Hibs were not only the first Scottish side to play in European competition, but also the first British side after Chelsea rejected the invitation. Eddie Turnbull, therefore, became the first British player to score in European competition. Turnbull himself added another, along with Lawrie Reilly and Willie Ormond. Hibs were to draw the return match 1-1 to qualify for the next round.

TUESDAY 15th SEPTEMBER 1992

Having qualified for the UEFA Cup by winning the League Cup the previous season, Hibs played Belgian cracks Anderlecht at a reduced-capacity Easter Road because of new rules regarding terracing. Anderlecht's squad boasted many stars of the future such as Danny Boffin, Marc Degryse, Peter van Vossen and Phillipe Albert. This first leg of the tie saw Hibs take the lead through Dave Beaumont after just four minutes, but Anderlecht equalised before the interval when they were awarded a soft penalty, which Degryse scored. Hibs kept attacking in the second half but were caught on the break, Van Vossen giving the visitors the lead. Mickey Weir was sent off, but midfield powerhouse Pat McGinlay levelled the tie at 2-2, then scored a third with a thunderbolt that crashed in off the bar, only to be inexplicably ruled out by the German referee, who claimed that the ball hadn't crossed the line. It finished 2-2, leaving Hibs a tough task for the second leg in Belgium because of the away-goals rule.

THURSDAY 15th SEPTEMBER 2005

Having qualified for the UEFA Cup after finishing third in the SPL the previous season, Hibs, celebrating 50 years since their first foray into European Competition, faced Ukrainian side Dnipro Dnipropetrovsk in this UEFA Cup first round, first leg tie at Easter Road. Radio Forth's Grant Stott was the MC on the 'mic' before the game, which finished 0-0, Hibs putting in a solid battling performance which seemed to bode well for the second leg.

WEDNESDAY 16th SEPTEMBER 1970

Hibs produced a stunning performance under manager Willie MacFarlane in this Fairs Cup first round first leg tie against Swedish side Malmo at Easter Road, in front of just under 12,000 fans. The Hibees destroyed the Swedes 6-0 on the night. Joe McBride scored a hat-trick, Arthur Duncan bagged a brace and the other goal came from Jim Blair, in what was an emphatic win for the Cabbage. Hibs went on to win the second leg in Sweden 3-2 with goals scored by Bobby Duncan, Pat Stanton and Billy McEwan, in front of only 1,900 fans. The final aggregate score was Hibs 9 Malmo 2.

SATURDAY 16th SEPTEMBER 1989

Hibs easily brushed aside St Mirren 3-1 at Easter Road in the league, with two goals from Keith Houchen, and one from John Collins. The Hibees would have scored more had it not been for the heroics of St Mirren goalie, Campbell Money. The Care Bears were a popular kids toy and TV 'thing' at the time, and for charity, there were two of these Care Bears, in full costumes, taking penalties at half-time. Hundreds of fans behind the goal and on the terracing were roaring 'SIGN THEM' as the 'bears' had their wee shoot-out.

WEDNESDAY 17th SEPTEMBER 1975

Hibs boss Eddie Turnbull vowed that Hibs would score at Anfield after the Hibees narrowly beat English giants Liverpool 1-0 in a UEFA Cup first round, first leg tie at Easter Road, in front of 20,000 fans. Liverpool 'keeper Ray Clemence saved a John Brownlie penalty and Liverpool had a goal chopped off. Joe Harper scored the only goal of the game.

SATURDAY 18th SEPTEMBER 1965

A remarkable Edinburgh derby at Tynecastle watched by 23,000 fans saw Hibs go 4-0 up in the first ten-minutes, so many latecomers to the match missed the goals, which were a brace apiece by Eric Stevenson and Jimmy O'Rourke. The game finished Hearts 0 Hibernian 4.

SATURDAY 18th SEPTEMBER 1971

There were 6,600 fans at Tannadice to see at Tannadice saw Eddie Turnbull's men crush the Arabs 4-1, with goals from Johnny Hamilton, Jimmy O'Rourke and a brace from Pat Stanton. Eric Stevenson came on as substitute in this game, his final appearance for the club. Signed from city-rivals Hearts in 1960, Stevenson played 390 times for Hibs in 11 years, scoring 79 goals. He moved to Ayr United from Hibernian.

SATURDAY 19th SEPTEMBER 1959

Hibs' young team failed to take the points at Cathkin Park against a more experienced Third Lanark side who would disappear from the Scottish game within ten years. Joe Baker was at the top of his form scoring twice for Hibs but 'Thirds' had scored five times past goalkeeper Willie Wilson before Johnny MacLeod scored a late consolation goal for the Cabbage. It finished 5-3 to Third Lanark. Hibs finished the season as top scorers in the league with 106 goals, more than champions Hearts. Unfortunately, the 85 goals conceded meant that they finished the season a lowly seventh in the league table.

WEDNESDAY 20th SEPTEMBER 1967

Bob Shankly's men were in Inter-Cities Fairs Cup (UEFA Cup) action at home against Portuguese giants FC Porto. 14,200 fans were at Easter Road for this first round first leg tie. Two first half goals by Peter Cormack and a second half strike by Eric Stevenson gave Hibs a comfortable 3-0 victory and a decent margin to defend in the second leg in Porto.

TUESDAY 21st SEPTEMBER 1993

Hibs were back at Tynecastle, a neutral venue once more, this time to play Ivan Golac's Dundee United side in the League-Cup semi-final. Hibs were looking to improve on their last semi-final match at Tynecastle, the 0-1 defeat in the Scottish Cup less than six months previously to Aberdeen. Once more, Hearts' 'shed' echoed with Hibs songs, from *Forever and Ever'* to *Glory Glory*. Hibs took an early lead through a sweet left-foot strike from the edge of the box by Darren Jackson, and the shed reverberated to a newer Hibs chant – *Ooh ah Jacksona!* – in the style of a Man Utd song about Eric Cantona. A fantastic display by Jim Leighton in the Hibs goal and some dogged work in defence and in midfield helped the Hibees hang on to the lead, despite sustained pressure by The Arabs, who had brought a large support down themselves. It finished 1-0 to Hibs, who would face the winner of the following day's Old-Firm semi-final, in the League Cup Final.

WEDNESDAY 22nd SEPTEMBER 1965

Already 2-0 up from the first leg at Recreation Park, Bob Shankly's Hibs took on Alloa Athletic in the League Cup quarter-final second leg at Easter Road. There was no fightback from the Wasps, as Hibernian crushed them 11-2 on the night to win 13-2 on aggregate. Two Hibs players scored four in this game, Jim Scott and Neil Martin, the Hibees' other goals coming from Pat Quinn, Eric Stevenson and a penalty from defender Joe Davis. Alloa's futile consolation efforts came from Marshall and Rutherford. Hibernian still hold the joint-record with Ayr United for goals scored in one game in the League Cup.

SATURDAY 23rd SEPTEMBER 1995

Alex Miller, often criticised for employing negative tactics when Hibs visited Glasgow, took his team to Ibrox to face Rangers in the league. Hibs got two things that were rare at Ibrox back then – a penalty and a win. Darren Jackson scored the only goal of the game from the penalty spot after 64 minutes, then Hibs survived the inevitable onslaught from the home-side to win the game 1-0 – Hibs' first win at Ibrox in five years.

TUESDAY 23rd SEPTEMBER 2003

In the League Cup second round, Hibs faced lowly Montrose at Easter Road. Bobby Williamson's side demolished the part-timers 9-0. Derek Riordan scored one of his trademark long-range wonder-goals, while Stephen Dobbie scored a hat-trick. Garry O'Connor (2), Ian Murray and Scott Brown also got onto the score-sheet, as did hapless Montrose defender Steve Kerrigan, with an own-goal.

SATURDAY 24th SEPTEMBER 1938

Willie McCartney was now showing signs of being on the brink of something special at Hibs, as the youngsters he was bringing into the Hibs team were starting to get results, like this one which was a resounding defeat of Aberdeen when they came to visit. Aberdeen had been viewed in some quarters as title contenders but they were thoroughly outclassed. The entire Hibs team were outstanding, and the game was over as a contest in the first quarter of an hour as Arthur Milne had scored twice and Sammy Kean added a third. Tommy McIntyre added a fourth before half-time, and after the break Milne completed his hat-trick so the match finished Hibernian 5 Aberdeen 0.

WEDNESDAY 25th SEPTEMBER 1985

Trailing 0-1 from the first leg at Ibrox, Hibs took on Rangers at Easter Road in the second leg of their League Cup semi-final, having already eliminated Celtic in the previous round. Rangers had beaten Hibs at Ibrox in the first leg thanks to a stunning effort from Davie Cooper. The two Gordons, Chisholm and Durie, scored for the Hibees to secure a second leg win of 2-0, Hibs going through to the final 2-1 on aggregate, where they would face Alex Ferguson's Aberdeen.

WEDNESDAY 25th SEPTEMBER 1991

Hibs took on the then-mighty Glasgow Rangers in the League Cup semi-final at Hampden Park, in front of just over 40,000 fans. Few outside Edinburgh gave the Hibees a chance against the champions, Hibs having recently been saved from extinction. A collision between Hibs striker Mark McGraw and Rangers' ex-Hibs 'keeper Andy Goram allowed Mickey Weir to cross to new signing Keith Wright, who headed past the two Rangers defenders on the line to put Hibs 1-0 up after 29 minutes. Hibs survived the next 61 minutes thanks to dogged defending and, against all odds, knocked the Glasgow giants out, 1-0. Hibs would face Dunfermline in the final, who had won the other semi-final, a tedious encounter at Tynecastle against Airdrieonians, after a penalty shoot-out.

TUESDAY 26th SEPTEMBER 1989

Hibs' first European foray in 11 years ended in triumph as the Easter Road men defeated Hungarian side Videoton 3-0 in Hungary, to win their UEFA Cup tie 4-0 on aggregate. Goals from Keith Houchen, Gareth Evans and John Collins completed the impressive display in front of 17,000 fans. Hibs had won the first leg at Easter Road 1-0 and were drawn to play Belgian side RFC Liege in the next round.

WEDNESDAY 27th SEPTEMBER 1972

Eddie Turnbull's Hibs side took on Portuguese giants Sporting Lisbon in a European Cup-Winners Cup first round, second leg tie at Easter Road in front of just under 27,000 fans. Hibs were 2-1 down from the first leg in Lisbon but went out and hammered Sporting 6-1 on the night to win 7-3 on aggregate. Hibs goals in the home win came courtesy of a Sporting own-goal, a brace from Alan Gordon and a hat-trick from Jimmy O'Rourke. Arthur Duncan had scored Hibs' solitary goal in the first leg defeat in Portugal, in front of 30,000 fans.

THURSDAY 27th SEPTEMBER 2001

Down 0-2 from the first leg in Greece, Hibs had a mountain to climb in their UEFA Cup second-leg against AEK Athens at Easter Road in front of a capacity crowd. Hibs initially did the unthinkable, scoring twice in the second-half through Francisco Javier Aguilera to take the tie into extra-time. Paco Luna (Aguilera's nick-name) even missed an open goal with the last touch of the 90 minutes. Greek danger-man Vassilis Tsartas was brought on by AEK and the Greeks were soon level on the night thanks to his brilliance, including a goal directly from a corner. A late David Zitelli wonder goal won the match 3-2 AET on the night for Hibs, but the Greek cracks - who have a habit of defeating British teams - went through 4-3 on aggregate. The match saw perhaps the most rousing recital of *Sunshine on Leith* ever seen or heard at Easter Road.

WEDNESDAY 28th SEPTEMBER 1977

Ewood Park was the venue for the Anglo-Scottish Cup quarter-final second leg between Blackburn Rovers and Hibernian. Eddie Turnbull's men had won the first leg 2-1 at Easter Road, and secured their place in the semi-finals by beating the English side 1-0 in Blackburn, thanks to a goal from Tony Higgins, in front of just over 6,000 fans. Hibernian were unlucky in the semi-final, losing 6-4 on aggregate to Bristol City, the tournament's eventual winners.

TUESDAY 29th SEPTEMBER 1992

Hibs slumped out of the UEFA Cup on away goals after drawing 1-1 with Belgian cracks Anderlecht in Brussels. Darren Jackson's goal cancelled out Luc Nilis' earlier strike but it wasn't enough for Alex Miller's men, who had drawn the first leg at Easter Road 2-2.

THURSDAY 29th SEPTEMBER 2005

Confident Hibs travelled to Ukraine to play the second leg of their UEFA Cup tie against Dnipro Dnipropetrovsk. Manager Tony Mowbray's inexperience as a manager at this level showed, as Hibs were utterly annihilated, Dnipro winning 5-1 on the night. Hibs' consolation goal came from Derek Riordan. One great positive to come out of the tie was the start of some great charity work by some Hibs fans, in the Hibs tradition, which in the years since has greatly helped Dnipro's many orphans and disadvantaged children.

TUESDAY 30th SEPTEMBER 1975

Anfield was the venue for Hibs' UEFA Cup first round second leg tie against Liverpool, Eddie Turnbull's men having taken a slim 1-0 advantage to Merseyside from the 1st leg in Edinburgh. It wasn't enough for Hibs, who lost 3-1 on the night, 3-2 on aggregate, in front of a crowd of just under 30,000. Pat Stanton was dropped for the match, in which Alex Edwards scored the Hibees' goal. John Toshack scored all three Liverpool goals.

MONDAY 30th SEPTEMBER 1996

A disastrous start to the season saw Alex Miller resign as Hibernian manager after almost ten years at the helm. His last game in charge was a 3-1 defeat at home to Hearts, an easy victory for the Jambos. Fans had been calling 'Miller must go' for years, yet he remains a divisive figure among Hibernian fans. He won the League Cup in 1991 and had gotten Hibs into Europe for the first time in a decade while he was in charge and also signed many of the fans' favourite players over the years. He was undoubtedly a good coach, but many argued that he lacked the personality to be a manager. The millstone around the neck of his tenure was the frustrating 22-match win-less run against city rivals Hearts from 1989 to 1994. Nevertheless, he is an iconic Hibernian boss. Hibs were mid-table when he left, and ended up finishing second bottom, only avoiding relegation via a play-off against Airdrie under new boss Jim Duffy that season. As with Pat Fenlon's departure in late 2013, for the Hibs fans, retrospectively, it was a case of 'be careful what you wish for'. Miller later went on to be Liverpool's assistant manager when they won the Champions League in 2005. On a final note, his statistics as Hibs boss show a curious thing – his 453 games in charge were just three games and nine goals away from creating an average result during his tenure of... 0-0!

HIBERNIAN FC
On This Day

OCTOBER

SATURDAY 1st OCTOBER 1910

Hibs maintained their position in the top three places in the league with this win against Hamilton Academical. The green jerseys were dominant in the first-half, and a goal after ten minutes by Harry Anderson from a cross by George Rae was entirely deserved. After the half-time break, Hibs continued to press and a second goal duly came from William Smith. Hamilton scored a late goal, and there was a nervy final spell to endure before Hibs held on to take both points.

WEDNESDAY 2nd OCTOBER 1974

There were 12,300 fans at Easter Road to see Hibs go head-to-head with Norwegian side Rosenborg in the UEFA Cup first round second leg. Hibs had won the first leg 3-2 in Norway and many predicted a close game in Edinburgh. Eddie Turnbull's side absolutely hammered the plucky part-timers 9-1 on the night, to go through 12-3 on aggregate. All the Hibees' goals in the 9-1 rout came from just five players. Iain Munro, Joe Harper and Pat Stanton bagged a brace apiece, while Alex Cropley scored two penalties. Alan Gordon also got on the scoresheet.

WEDNESDAY 3rd OCTOBER 1962

Just 4,000 fans watched Walter Galbraith's Hibernian side play Denmark's KB Copenhagen in the Fairs Cup first round first leg. Hibs bulldozed the Danes 4-0 on the night with goals from John Byrne, Gerry Baker, Morris Stevenson and an own goal by Copenhagen's Ronnow, all in the first half. Another 40,00 crowd saw a more competitive game in Denmark for the second leg, Hibs winning 3-2 in Copenhagen thanks to a double from Morris Stevenson and a strike by John Byrne. The Hibees went through 7-2 on aggregate.

MONDAY 3rd OCTOBER 1988

Skipper Gordon Rae's testimonial saw Manchester United visit Easter Road. This game is best remembered for Joe Tortolano being red-carded in the opening minutes for a horrid tackle on United's Gordon Strachan, a Hibs fan. 14,000 fans turned up to pay tribute to Rae, the match ended in a 3-0 victory for the visitors, whose goals came from David Wilson, Mark Hughes and Mark Robins.

SATURDAY 3rd OCTOBER 1998

The Shyberry Excelsior Stadium, Airdrieonians' new ground, played host to this division one encounter, the first between Hibs and The Diamonds since the Hibees had annihilated them in the season 1996/97 relegation play-off. Ex-Hearts man Kenny Black scored a penalty for Airdrie, but Hibs came out on top 3-1 winners, with a goal from Mixu Paatelainen and a brace from Pat McGinlay.

WEDNESDAY 4th OCTOBER 1967

Hibs made the trip to Portugal for the second leg of their Fairs Cup 1st round tie against FC Porto. 40,000 fans watched as the Hibees set out their stall to defend their 3-0 advantage from the first leg. Peter Cormack, hero of the 1st leg, was sent off in the first half, as was Porto's Rolando. A brace from Valdir and a goal by Pinto had Hibs worried, but a late penalty from Joe Davis sealed the Hibees' place in the next round, Porto winning the second leg 3-1 on the night, but Hibernian winning the tie 4-3 on aggregate.

SATURDAY 4th OCTOBER 1997

Playing with confidence and swagger and doing well in the league, Hibs welcomed champions Rangers to Easter Road for a league match. The Govan side opened the scoring with a Marco Negri penalty-kick, but Pat McGinlay and Barry Lavety goals put Hibs 2-1 up at half-time. In a pulsating match where Rangers played their usual physical game but also showed some good skill, Hibs were nevertheless in the ascendancy. Stevie Crawford nodded the ball past Theo Snelders just after half-time, putting Hibs 3-1 up and seemingly in complete control. Hibs fans were jubilant. Rangers ended that jubilation by replying with a Paul Gascoigne free-kick, a Jorg Albertz pile-driver and another goal from Marco Negri to win the match 4-3 in the end. For Hibs, this game was a disaster. It seemed to knock the stuffing out of Jim Duffy and his team, who lost their confidence after it and never recovered it until it was too late in the season. This defeat, ultimately, began Hibs' sad journey towards relegation.

SATURDAY 5th OCTOBER 1963

A seven-goal thriller at Fir Park in the league saw Walter Galbraith's Hibs team edged out, losing 4-3 to Motherwell. An Andy Weir penalty and a hat-trick from Joe McBride being enough to keep the two points in Lanarkshire, despite Hibernian's three strikes from Gerry Baker, Neil Martin, and a goal on his debut for a certain Patrick Stanton, in front of a crowd of around 6400.

SATURDAY 6th OCTOBER 2007

John Collins took his Hibs team to Ibrox in the SPL. David Murphy scored the only goal of the game, Hibs winning 1-0 and going top of the league. For long periods of the match, Hibs' fast, skilful passing game style had Rangers chasing shadows, to jubilant cries of 'ole' from the small band of away supporters.

WEDNESDAY 7th OCTOBER 1964

Jock Stein's Hibs side took on Spanish giants Real Madrid at Easter Road, in a friendly match. In reality, there was nothing remotely 'friendly' going on on the pitch, as both sides fielded strong teams and played as if it were indeed a competitive match. In front of 30,000 fans, Hibs defeated Real Madrid 2-0, thanks to goals from 19-year-old Peter Cormack and Real's Zoco, who scored an own-goal. There was a good-natured pitch invasion at the end, Hibs fans clearly being overjoyed at beating the Spaniards.

SATURDAY 8th OCTOBER 1994

Hibs took on Rangers at Easter Road in the league, and went 1-0 down after just ten minutes when big Basile Boli headed in a Brian Laudrup cross. For some reason Rangers moved striker Mark Hateley to centre-back in the second half. A pinpoint Michael O'Neill free-kick from the edge of the box, which should actually have been given as a penalty, was nevertheless stabbed in at the back post by skipper Gordon Hunter to make it 1-1 after 46 minutes. Hibs played the final 30 minutes with SIX forwards, and it paid-off with just eight minutes to go, when another magical ball from O'Neill was headed past Andy Goram by Kevin Harper to give Alex Miller's men a 2-1 win.

WEDNESDAY 9th OCTOBER 1968

Hibernian reached the Scottish League Cup Final by beating Dundee 2-1 at neutral Tynecastle in the semi-final, watched by just under 20,000 fans. Hibs' goals came from Allan McGraw and Colin Stein.

WEDNESDAY 9th OCTOBER 1974

Hibs defeated Falkirk 1-0 at Tynecastle, a neutral venue for this League Cup semi-final. Joe Harper scored the game's only goal, in front of just under 20,000 fans. Hibs would face Celtic in the final.

SATURDAY 10th OCTOBER 1987

10,000 fans at Easter Road saw Hibs crush Dunfermline Athletic 4-0, goals coming from Eddie May, Paul Kane, George McCluskey and John Collins. Scotland's second choice 'keeper Andy Goram made his Hibs debut in this league match, aged 23, following his £325,000 move from Oldham Athletic. Goram is widely regarded as one of Hibernian's greatest ever goalkeepers. He played 163 games for Hibs between 1987 and 1991, being sold to Rangers in 1991 for £1m and going on to be a legend there and for Scotland, later even playing for Manchester United. He scored twice for Hibs, once from a clearance-kick, once in a penalty shoot-out. Many a time, particularly in derbies, Goram saved Hibs from heavy defeats with his heroics.

SAURDAY 11th OCTOBER 1952

'BULL'S EYE TURNBULL' was the headline in the *Glasgow Evening Times* as the Famous Five ensured that Hibs recorded a famous victory at Ibrox. Rangers took the lead in the 21st minute, but it was not to be a lead they held for long as Willie Ormond crossed for Eddie Turnbull to lay off to Lawrie Reilly who levelled the scores eight minutes later. Hibs had been the more polished team, although they did not have the advantage until the closing minutes when Eddie Turnbull scored a wonder goal for Hibs, with a sensational shot from outside the penalty box after Gordon Smith and Lawrie Reilly had set up the chance. A crowd of 65,000 had turned up at Ibrox to see an excellent game between the two dominant sides of the post-war period in Scotland.

SATURDAY 12th OCTOBER 1996

With Alex Miller having resigned after ten years at the helm, Hibs were under the temporary charge of Jocky Scott, playing Rangers at Easter Road in the league. Jorg Albertz blasted the 'Gers into the lead after just nine minutes with a stunning free-kick that left Jim Leighton helpless. Hibs came out fighting in the second half, Harper and Jackson terrorising the Rangers defence. Hibs were awarded a penalty on the hour, which Darren Jackson duly slammed into the corner to level things at 1-1, to cries of 'Ooh-ah Jackson-a!' from the Hibs supporters. Hibs then took the lead through a close-range effort by Graeme Donald just three minutes later, and held on to win the match 2-1, despite Rangers being awarded a late penalty. Brian Laudrup missed the spot-kick, only for the referee to order it to be re-taken, so Laudrup had another go and this time, the outstanding Jim Leighton saved it. After the game, many Hibs players stated that they would like to see Jocky Scott get the manager's job on a full-time basis, but he never got it.

SUNDAY 12th OCTOBER 1997

Craig Levein's SECOND testimonial for Hearts was played at Tynecastle, with Hibs the visitors. Levein's first testimonial in 1995 had been attended by just 3,000 fans, but just under 9,000 fans came along to this game. Hibs won 1-0 thanks to a goal by 19-year-old Andrew Newman. Rumours that Rugby star and Hearts fan Gavin Hastings would be playing for Hearts in this match proved untrue, but Hibs' squad featured TV's John Leslie, and former Hibs star John Collins. Hearts' squad featured several of Levein's old team-mates.

SATURDAY 13th OCTOBER 1894

After winning the second division the year before, but failing to win promotion due to the rules of election at the time, Hibs had kicked off the following season in the same fashion and were dominating the league. On this day they ventured to Morton and were victors by the impressive tally of seven goals to one. Arthur Brady was in particularly good form, and helped himself to a hat-trick. Hibs scored 92 goals in their 18 league matches at an average of more than four goals per game that season, and won the league from Motherwell by eight points.

MONDAY 14th OCTOBER 1963

Walter Galbraith's Hibs team were knocked out of the League Cup at the semi-final stage 1-0 by Greenock Morton, in a replay at Ibrox watched by around 37,000 fans, Allan McGraw scoring the only goal of the game from the penalty-spot. The first game at Ibrox a week before had ended 1-1, Hibs goal coming from Neil Martin. Over 45,000 had watched the first game.

SUNDAY 15th OCTOBER 2006

Caretaker boss Mark Venus took charge of Hibernian for the first and only time, as Hibs hosted city-rivals Hearts in the league, following the departure of Tony Mowbray to West Brom. 16,600 fans saw Hibs race into a two-goal lead, Zemmama scoring with a sweet strike after just five minutes, then Chris Killen doubling the lead with a header after 16 minutes. Andrius Velicka pulled one back for Hearts before the interval. Mikoliunas was sent-off for Hearts after 59 minutes, leading to Hibs taking the ascendancy in the game, Hearts' 'keeper Craig Gordon saving the ten-man Jambos from annihilation with a string of saves. Hibernian then contrived to throw the win away, Velicka equalising for Hearts with a goal that was largely the fault of Hibs' 'keeper Malkowski, who had also been to blame for Hearts' first goal. Despite late pressure from Hibs, Hearts held on to earn a 2-2 draw. Mark Proctor managed Hibs on an interim basis for the club's next two matches, before fans' favourite John Collins was given the manager's job.

SATURDAY 16th OCTOBER 1909

Hibs enjoyed success at Hampden Park, beating Queens Park in a league game in front of a crowd of 10,000 supporters – a crowd the Spiders would be delighted to see in current times. In this entertaining game both sides played brightly, and the standard was impressive. Hibs had the better of the play, but they fell behind to the amateurs when they gave away a soft headed goal by Bowie. Parity was restored before half-time when William Smith scored. The game was even in the second-half, but Hibs took the points with a well worked corner from Donald Dixon who found the head of Hugh Logan to score the winner. This was some consolation for Logan who had had a first-half effort ruled out.

SATURDAY 17th OCTOBER 1987

Alex Miller got his first ever victory in an Edinburgh derby, as Hibs beat Hearts 2-1 at Easter Road. All of the goals came in the first half, John Robertson equalising Eddie May's early strike, with Paul Kane netting what turned out to be the winner after 41 minutes.

MONDAY 18th OCTOBER 2010

Hibernian appointed former Scotland international Colin Calderwood as manager, John Hughes having left Easter Road after a very disappointing start to the season, despite finishing fourth in the league and qualifying for Europe in the previous season, his first season in the Hibs hot-seat. It was not to prove a good switch for the Easter Road faithful. Asides the brief but disastrous reign of Terry Butcher, Calderwood was the worst Hibs boss since the club had been promoted in 1999. His Hibs team lost its first three games with him in charge, and his only real achievement at Hibs was a surprise victory over Rangers at Ibrox. Calderwood managed Hibs in 49 games, the Hibees winning 12, drawing 11 and losing 26, scoring just 53 goals. Pat Fenlon was brought in as manager late in 2011 to save the club from relegation, which he managed to do.

SATURDAY 19th OCTOBER 1996

Hibs travelled to Fir Park to play Motherwell on league business under caretaker boss Jocky Scott, having just beaten Rangers 2-1 at Easter Road. Hibs' goalie Jim Leighton was sent-off for the first time in his career, after accidentally handling the ball outside his area. Hibs' defensive midfielder Andy Millen picked up Leighton's gloves and took over in goal, as Hibs had no goalkeeper on the bench. Hibernian had been leading 1-0 before Leighton's dismissal thanks to a Kevin Harper goal. Hibs formed a 'ring of steel' around their vulnerable 'goalkeeper' and defended well, holding on until the 75th minute, when Shaun McSkimming finally equalised for Motherwell. It finished 1-1. Chris Reid replaced the suspended Leighton in Hibs' next match, a 0-4 drubbing from Celtic at Parkhead.

SATURDAY 20th OCTOBER 1883

Hibs have had many titanic encounters with their local rivals Heart of Midlothian, especially in the early years of the Scottish Cup. Hibs trounced their rivals 4-1 in this cup game, and the contemporary reports of the time give some idea of the changes that have occurred in football in the intervening 130 years. Hearts had been expected to win as they had been in much better form, and newspaper reports tell us the game was more physical than expected and several of the players were paying more attention to making contact with opposing players rather than the ball! James McGhee scored twice for Hibs, and Jim Brogan and Tommy Lee scored the others. *The Scotsman* described the attendance as 'an assemblage estimated at between 6,000 and 7,000'.

SATURDAY 21st OCTOBER 2001

A 5.35pm Edinburgh Derby kick-off time for SKY TV saw a boisterous Hibs support truly show the meaning of the phrase 'the 12th man'. Hibs raced into an early two-goal lead with a brace from Ecuadorian wing-back Ulises De La Cruz, and every time Hearts got the ball the East Stand rang with boos and jeers. Hearts gave up, and though they pulled one back in the second half through Stephen Simmons, the result was never in doubt. At the final whistle, Hibs players led by Franck Sauzee ran over to the middle of the East Stand, to give THE FANS a standing ovation.

SUNDAY 22nd OCTOBER 2000

The live televised Edinburgh derby at Easter Road saw Andy Kirk and Colin Cameron score for Hearts – either side of six goals from rampant Hibs, including a hat-trick from Finnish striker Mixu Paatelainen and a gem of a goal by Russell Latapy. Hibs' other goals were scored by John O'Neil and David Zitelli. One of the loudest cheers of the night came when Cameron scored for Hearts late on to make it 6-2, though most of those who sarcastically cheered were in the Hibs end.

WEDNESDAY 23rd OCTOBER 1912

Edinburgh's teams both enjoyed a successful night in the Inter City Midweek League games. Hearts defeated Rangers 3-0 at Tynecastle in front of 4,000 fans, while Hibernian, playing with an outfield player in goal, managed an impressive 2-0 win over in-form Aberdeen at Pittodrie.

WEDNESDAY 23rd OCTOBER 1974

An Old Lady visited Easter Road, in the shape of Italian giants Juventus for a UEFA Cup second round first leg tie. Hibernian led 2-1 at one point in the match thanks to Alex Cropley and Pat Stanton strikes, but were eventually overwhelmed on the night, losing 4-2 in front of nearly 30,000 fans. The second leg in Turin was a harsh footballing lesson for the men from Leith, who were hammered 4-0, losing the tie 8-2 on aggregate.

SATURDAY 23rd OCTOBER 1999

Dundee visited Leith on league business and were thrashed 5-2 by Alex Mcleish's side. Hibs goals came from a Russell Latapy double, Franck Sauzee, Kenny Miller and from substitute Dirk Lehman. Hibs had now scored nine goals in two games against the Dens men.

SUNDAY 24th OCTOBER 1993

Hibs took on Rangers in the League Cup Final at Celtic Park, aiming to win the trophy for the second time in two years. Despite a valiant effort, the Easter Road men lost the thrilling match 2-1 after a late wonder-goal by Ally McCoist. Ian Durrant had given the Ibrox side the lead just after half-time, but an own-goal by former Hearts player Dave McPherson after perseverance from Keith Wright had deservedly levelled the match, before McCoist's audacious overhead kick took the cup back to Ibrox. Comedian Andy Cameron and TV's Mr Blobby took to the pitch to celebrate with the Rangers players, but Hibs got the last word, with most of the 18,000 Hibbies on the terrace behind the goal staying behind to sing *You'll Never Walk Alone*, with scarves, and heads, held high.

WEDNESDAY 25th OCTOBER 1972

The Hibees' adventure in the Cup Winners Cup continued in this second round 1st leg tie against Albanian side Besa Kavaje in Edinburgh, in front of just under 23,000 fans. Eddie Turnbull's men destroyed the Albanians 7-1, with goals from John Brownlie, Alex Cropley, a brace from Arthur Duncan and another hat-trick in the competition from Jimmy O'Rourke putting the tie beyond doubt before the second leg. Hibernian drew the second leg 1-1 in Albania in front of 20,000 fans, Alan Gordon equalising for Hibs after Pagria had given the home side the lead. Hibs won 8-2 on aggregate and progressed to the quarter-finals. Besa and Hibs were clearly light-years apart on the pitch, but did have one thing in common – both clubs were in the Cup Winners Cup despite not actually winning their country's cup the previous season, having both qualified as runners-up.

SATURDAY 26th OCTOBER 1964

54,000 fans were at Hampden to see Hibs take on Celtic in the League Cup Final, in what has went down as one of Scottish football's greatest games. Joe Harper gained the honour of scoring a hat-trick for Hibs in a Cup Final. Alas for Eddie Turnbull's men, another player scored a hat-trick in this game, Celtic's Dixie Deans, who had also scored a treble against Hibs in a league match the week before. Jimmy Johnstone had given the Hoops an early lead. Hibs battled well but it seemed that everytime the Hibees edged back into the match with one of Harper's goals, Celtic responded by upping their game. The thrilling match ended Hibs 3 Celtic 6. The attendance was so low because of a series of nationwide strikes.

SUNDAY 27th OCTOBER 1985

John Blackley's Hibs team took on Aberdeen in the League Cup Final at Hampden in front of over 40,000 fans. Sadly for those in green and white who made the trip west, Hibs froze on the day and lost the final 0-3, Billy Stark and Eric Black(2) scoring for the 'Dons. Hibs efforts on goal were restricted to a solitary strike by Paul Kane.

SUNDAY 27th OCTOBER 1991

Alex Miller's men, having conquered Rangers in the semi-final, faced Dunfermline Athletic in the League Cup Final at Hampden Park. A dull first half saw Hibs receive a half-time 'roasting' from Alex Miller, and it worked. Hibs were all-over the Pars in the second half, Mickey Weir in particular giving Dunfermline defenders Ray Sharp and Davie Moyes a torrid time, and Hibs took the lead from a coolly taken Tommy McIntrye spot-kick, after Weir had been fouled in the box. Weir then provided a great through ball which completely outfoxed Davie Moyes and sent Keith Wright clear through on goal, Wright slotting the ball past Pars 'keeper Andy Rhodes into the net. Hibs won 2-0, and picked up their first major trophy since 1972. Keith Wright had scored in every round.

THURSDAY 28th OCTOBER 1965

Franck Sauzee was born, in Aubenas, France. The midfielder enjoyed a successful career in the French and Italian leagues, the greatest achievement of which was when he was part of the Marseille team who won the first ever Champions League in 1993. Alex McLeish signed him on a 'free' from Montpelier in February 1999, and he made his debut, aged 33, in the somewhat Spartan surroundings of Falkirk's Brockville Stadium in a 2-1 win for the Hibees. He oozed class and soon became a fans' favourite as Hibs stormed their way to the division one title and promotion in 1999, and was again a hero in the following season as Hibs cemented their return to the top-flight and reached the semi-finals of the Scottish Cup. He is best remembered for his trademark long-range efforts and free-kicks, which accounted for many of the 16 goals he scored in his time at Easter Road, and also for his contribution to several important derby-wins, the big Frenchman never losing to Hearts either as a player or as a manager. He played as sweeper in the 2000/01 season in which Hibernian finished third and reached the Scottish Cup Final, qualifying for Europe. He had an ill-fated spell as Hibs boss following the departure of Alex Mcleish the following season, which is best forgotten, but despite that, he is a cult-hero to Hibs fans, his place in Hibby hearts being summed up by the iconic chant 'There's Only One Sauzee'. Sauzee also played for France 39 times, scoring nine goals, but only ever played at the 1992 European Championships under Michel Platini, as France failed to qualify for USA '94.

SATURDAY 29th OCTOBER 1994

Alex Miller's men beat Hearts for the second time in three months, winning 2-1 at Easter Road thanks to two goals in three first half minutes from Darren Jackson and Michael O'Neill. John Robertson netted a late consolation for the Jambos from the penalty-spot. At this game, Hearts fans sat in the seated but uncovered Dunbar End and had to be issued with luminous yellow waterproof ponchos, because of torrential rain.

SATURDAY 29th OCTOBER 2005

Singing 'We are unbeatable', Hearts fans made the trip to Easter Road to play Tony Mowbray's Hibs team. Hearts were indeed

GUILLAUME BEUZELIN CELEBRATES WITH BENJI AFTER WINNING THE 2007 CUP FINAL unbeaten in the league, and had thumped Hibs 4-0 at Tynecastle earlier in the season, but crucially, their manager George Burley had just resigned after falling out with owner Vladimir Romanov. Hibs won the match 2-0 with second half goals coming from Guillaume Beuzelin and Garry O'Connor. Hearts had Jankauskas sent-off midway through the second half. It turned out, Hearts weren't 'unbeatable'.

WEDNESDAY 30th OCTOBER 1968

Striker David Zitelli was born, in Mont-Saint-Martin, France. The 31 year-old striker was signed by Alex Mcleish in 2000 just before Didier Agathe's untimely departure to Celtic. Prior to joining Hibs, Zitelli was best known to British fans for his double against Liverpool in the 1997 UEFA Cup, as his club Strasbourg knocked out the Merseyside club. Zitelli played 64 times for Hibs, around half of them after coming off the bench, and he scored 13 goals, most of them beauties, including a goal in the 6-2 win against Hearts in 2000, a week after he had scored the only goal in Hibs 1-0 victory over Rangers at Easter Road. A stunning tight-angle strike against Motherwell in a win at Fir Park, an overhead kick in a win against Dundee at Dens Park, a Scottish Cup semi-final goal against Livingston and a breathtaking 'on the night' winner against AEK Athens at Easter Road in 2001. He left Hibs for Istre in early 2002, and though he wasn't at Hibs very long, he remains a cult-hero among the Easter Road faithful.

SATURDAY 30th OCTOBER 1993

After the previous week's disappointment against Rangers in the League Cup Final, Hibs were looking to bounce back and continue their fine league form, against Hearts at Easter Road. Hearts had been struggling in the league, in contrast to Hibs' good start that season. Almost predictably, Hearts won the match easily, 2-0, with two goals from John Colquhoun, the pick of which was a 36-yard lob over Jim Leighton. Hibs still looked jaded from their exertions in the Cup Final a week earlier. Amid a poisonous atmosphere, the Hearts fans spent most of the match singing 'Super Ally' repeatedly, in reference to Ally McCoist's winning goal for Rangers against Hibs the previous week.

TUESDAY 31st OCTOBER 1989

The Stade Jules Georges was the venue for the Hibees' UEFA Cup second round, second leg tie against RFC Liege. The first leg at Easter Road had finished 0-0, with Keith Houchen having missed a penalty. Hibs battled and competed well against the Belgian side, and after 90 minutes the tie was still all-square at 0-0. Alas for Hibs, it just wasn't to be, when in the 105th minute Jean-François De Sart smashed an unstoppable long-range effort past the helpless Andy Goram in the Hibs goal. It finished 1-0 to Liege on aggregate, and Alex Miller's men were out.

HIBERNIAN FC
On This Day

NOVEMBER

WEDNESDAY 1st NOVEMBER 1978

Trailing 2-0 from the first leg in France, Hibs took on French cracks Strasbourg in this UEFA Cup second round second leg tie at Easter Road, watched by fewer than 14,000 fans. Eddie Turnbull's side were unable to progress to the next round, but won the match 1-0 on the night thanks to a penalty by Ally McLeod. Strasbourg won the tie 2-1 on aggregate. Hibs had disposed of Swedish side IFK Norrkoping 3-2 on aggregate in the 1st round, all of the tie's goals, including a double from Tony Higgins, coming in the 1st leg at Easter Road.

SATURDAY 2nd NOVEMBER 1963

Willie Hamilton made his debut for Hibernian. It wasn't the best of starts, as Walter Galbraith's side lost 2-1 to Partick Thistle at Firhill, Peter Cormack scoring for the Hibees. Hamilton, signed from Hearts in 1963, played 74 times for Hibs, scoring 24 goals. He also played for Scotland once. He left Hibs for Aston Villa in 1965 but later sustained serious injuries in a car-crash, later returning to play for Hearts in 1967.

SATURDAY 3rd NOVEMBER 1973

Over 9,000 at Easter Road saw Turnbull's Tornadoes thump Clyde 5-0, in a league match. John Blackley and Alex Cropley got on the scoresheet, but the star of this one-sided game was Pat Stanton, who bagged a superb hat-trick with a long-range effort, a diving header and a penalty. The Bully Wee were shell-shocked.

WEDNESDAY 3rd NOVEMBER 1993

Plans for a 20,000-seater stadium to be leased by Hibs on a 100-acre site at Straiton adjacent to the Edinburgh City Bypass were submitted for planning permission to Midlothian District Council today. The first phase of the stadium development was expected to cost around £8 million and involve 12,000 seats, with two other phases to follow. Mr Douglas Cromb, Chairman of Hibs at the time, said it was expected that work would begin on the new ground the following summer and that Hibernian would be able to move from Easter Road in time for the start of the 1994/95 season, to comply with the Taylor Report.

SATURDAY 4th NOVEMBER 2006

Former Hibs midfielder John Collins took charge of Hibernian as manager for the first time, as the replacement for the departed Tony Mowbray. The Hibees had been managed by Mark Venus and Mark Proctor on an interim basis until Collins' arrival. Over 13,000 fans were at Easter Road for the match against Kilmarnock. A Shelton Martis own-goal just after half-time gave Killie the lead, but Hibs were 2-1 up just eight minutes later, hitting back with goals from Michael Stewart and Steven Fletcher. Stevie Naismith equalised for Kilmarnock after 65 minutes, capitalising on a goalkeeping error by Malkowski. It finished 2-2. Hibs, and Collins, faced a tough test in their next match – a League Cup quarter-final at home to Hearts.

SATURDAY NOVEMBER 5th 1949

In one of many titanic battles between the clubs in the post-war era, Hibs defeated Rangers 1-0 and thereby ended the Ibrox club's unbeaten league run since the start of the season. In front of one of the biggest crowds ever seen at Easter Road – 51,000 – Hibs played the better football, but it was the visitors who created the better chances. However, goals win games and the only one in this fixture was scored by Hibs left-winger Eddie Turnbull, on the hour mark. Hibs were served well by all of the Famous Five and also by half-back Jock Paterson – father of current media pundit Craig.

SATURDAY 6th NOVEMBER 1965

Hamilton Accies visited Easter Road to take on Bob Shankly's men in the league, in front of around 6,300 fans. Hamilton managed to score twice, though one of their efforts was an own-goal. Luckily for the Easter Road faithful, the Cabbage smashed an additional TEN goals past Accies, to win the match 11-1, equalling Hibs' all-time highest league victory, an 11-1 win against Airdrieonians in 1959. In this Easter Road rout, Hibernian's goals came from Davie Hogg, Peter Cormack, Joe Davis, Accies' own goal, a brace apiece from Jim Scott and Jimmy O'Rourke and a hat-trick from man of the match Eric Stevenson.

WEDNESDAY 7th NOVEMBER 1973

After a goal-less draw in the first leg of their second round UEFA Cup tie against Leeds Utd at Elland Road two weeks previously, Eddie Turnbull's Hibs again drew 0-0 with the English side in the 2nd leg at Easter Road. Extra-time produced no goals and the tie went to penalties, Hibs losing 5-4 in the shoot-out, Pat Stanton being the 'sinner', blasting Hibs' 1st penalty against the post.

WEDNESDAY 8th NOVEMBER 2006

John Collins took charge of Hibs for the second time since replacing Tony Mowbray as manager for this home League Cup quarter-final against Hearts. Hibs fans were hungry for revenge after losing to Hearts in the other cup at Hampden only six months earlier. Revenge was sweet as the Hibees won the match 1-0, thanks to a powerful shot by defender Rob Jones. Rather than run up a huge scoreline, Hibs settled for giving Hearts a lesson in possession football, the Gorgie side chasing shadows for much of the match. Hibs had the ball for 81% of the game, and deservedly earned their place in the semi-final.

SATURDAY 9th NOVEMBER 1889

Hibs were a team in decline, when they visited Dumfries on Scottish Cup fourth round duty on this day. Heavily plundered by Celtic, their cup winning team of only two years earlier was now a distant memory and worse days would follow. However, this game went well for the Hibees, despite strong resistance from the home team, and Hibs finally prevailed by 7-3 against Queen of the South Wanderers.

SATURDAY 10th NOVEMBER 1990

Hibernian played their first ever match at McDiarmid Park, St Johnstone's new stadium, the first new purpose built football stadium in the UK. St Johnstone's previous home in Perth had been Muirton Park. A near capacity crowd witnessed a tepid affair, Alex Miller's struggling side earning a 1-1 draw, Hibs' goal coming from Paul Wright, a player who after being sold would later come back to haunt Hibs during his spells at St Johnstone and Kilmarnock.

WEDNESDAY 10th NOVEMBER 2010

Colin Calderwood's Hibs team faced a stern test – a midweek tie against champions Rangers at Ibrox. In perhaps the only result of Calderwood's tenure worthy of remembrance, Hibs, playing in yellow, stunned the Ibrox legions, easily beating Walter Smith's team 3-0, with goals from Liam Miller, John Rankin and Francis Dickoh.

SATURDAY 11th NOVEMBER 1882

Before the days of league action, which was still several years off, the Scottish Cup was the only national competition in Scottish football and on this day Hibs entertained Glasgow side Partick Thistle at Easter Road, in front of a crowd of around 2,000. Malachy Byrne of the original Hibs side from 1875 was still playing, and long serving Owen Brannigan featured in this match. The match was noted as being more physical than normal, but finished 2-2. The replay the following week in Glasgow was won by Hibs by the more comfortable margin of 4-1. Hibs were eventually knocked out by Arthurlie, losing 6-0 after a disputed and replayed 4-3 defeat.

SATURDAY 12th NOVEMBER 1988

Hearts hadn't lost to Hibs at Tynecastle for ten years, but that hoodoo ended in this Edinburgh Derby. Hibs scored first through Paul Kane, but then had skipper Gordon Rae sent-off. Despite being down to ten-men, Hibs held on, then in 83 minutes, a sublime flick from Kane put striker Steve Archibald through on goal, leaving Hearts' Dave McPherson trailing in his wake as he smashed the ball into Henry Smith's bottom corner at the Gorgie Road end from 22 yards to make it 2-0 to Hibs, to the utter elation of the Hibs fans on the Gorgie Road Terrace behind the goal. Dave McPherson netted an injury-time consolation for Hearts, and it finished 2-1.

WEDNESDAY 13th NOVEMBER 1968

Bob Shankly had inherited a fine side from Jock Stein, and they achieved some notable performances as well as results. In this second round Inter City Fairs Cup, first leg they met the crack East-German side Lokomotiv Leipzig. Hibs produced another of their fine European performances, which Joe McBride senior capped by becoming the first Hibs player to score a hat-trick in European competition. A solitary strike by Hans-Jorg Naumann meant that Hibs headed behind the Iron Curtain defending a 3-1 lead. Hibs forward Alex Scott took exception to some of the rough tackling of the opponents and was ordered off the field after retaliating against the East German left-back Peter Giessner.

SATURDAY 14th NOVEMBER 1992

Jim Jefferies' Falkirk visited Easter Road on a freezing afternoon, on league business. Gary Lennox gave the Bairns the lead with a looping effort after 12 minutes. Joe Tortolano equalised for the Hibees just one minute later, to cries of 'Joe, Joe , Super Joe' from the terracing. Falkirk had a string of chances to score before the interval, but a combination of their own inept finishing and splendid goalkeeping from John Burridge kept things level at half-time. Hibs improved after the break but Falkirk kept going forward, Burridge denying the Bairns another goal with more great saves, then Gareth Evans scored for Hibernian with a header after 67 minutes. Substitute Brian Hamilton scored in the last minute to give the Hibees a somewhat fortunate 3-1 win, in front of just over 7,000 fans.

SATURDAY 15th NOVEMBER 1980

Willie Ormond took charge of Hibernian for the last time, as the Hibees took on Hamilton Accies at Easter Road in the first division. Ormond was quitting because of poor health. The match was actually a thrilling 3-3 draw, for the neutral, Hibs' goals coming courtesy of a brace from Ally MacLeod, one of which was a penalty, and a strike from Gordon Rae. Ormond, a legend as a player at Hibernian, was replaced by Bertie Auld, another ex-player, who ultimately got Hibs promoted that season. Just 3,600 fans made it to this game.

SATURDAY 16th NOVEMBER 1878

The Scottish Cup third round draw threw up a local derby for Hibernian as they were drawn to play Edinburgh University at their Corstorphine Sports Grounds. The match was eagerly anticipated by the Edinburgh football public, and a special train was put on from Waverley to Corstorphine and the crowd numbered several hundred in these embryonic football times in Edinburgh. A splendid match saw the Hibs prevail by 5-2, with Frank Rourke scoring a hat-trick. Hibs founder Michael Whelehan played in goals for Hibs, and the 'heavy and unnecessary charging' which Hibs' play the previous season had become known for was nowhere to be seen.

SATURDAY 17th NOVEMBER 1934

Hibs visited Somerset Park on league business, against a recently strengthened Ayr United side. Bobby Templeton's Hibs side was best served by half-back Willie Watson and their young and energetic forwards who battled all game. Ayr had taken a first-half lead which they were carrying into the later stages, but Hibs never gave up and it was deserving of their efforts when Rab Walls scored the equalising goal in the last minute of the game, for the match to finish 1-1 and Hibs to leave with a share of the points. It has to be said, Hibernian goalkeeper John Hill played his part too.

SATURDAY 18th NOVEMBER 2006

Another one of those periodic high-scoring Hibs v Motherwell games at Fir Park saw John Collins and his team utterly destroy the Steelmen, in a league match. The men in claret and amber had no answer to the Total Football that the Hibees displayed, Collins having improved the departed Tony Mowbray's already good team by insisting on an even more direct, slick, passing game style and a much tighter defensive mentality at the back. Hibs were 4-0 up at half-time thanks to goals from Chris Killen, Scott Brown and a brace from Ivan Sproule. Rob Jones and Dean Shiels completed the rout in the second half, Stephen McGarry netting Motherwell's futile consolation with seven minutes remaining. It finished Motherwell 1 Hibs 6.

SATURDAY 19th NOVEMBER 1983

Manager Pat Stanton and just over 4,000 fans saw Hibernian take on St Johnstone at Easter Road in the league. A Willie Irvine hat-trick and a goal by Arthur Duncan helped Hibs to an easy 4-1 win over the Perthshire side. Hibs' Bobby Thomson was sent-off in this game for running 50 yards to deck a linesman, an act which earned the notorious hot-head a six-month ban! It wasn't the first time that Thomson had come to blows with an official in his career.

SATURDAY 20th NOVEMBER 2004

Just over 5,000 fans at Dens Park saw Tony Mowbray's men take on Dundee in the league. Hibs were 2-0 up at half-time thanks to goals from Beuzelin and Derek Riordan. Steve Lovell pulled one back for Dundee on the hour mark, but as a match, this really was no contest, the Dark Blues chasing shadows against Mowbray's team's slick passing game. Alen Orman and Dean Shiels completed the rout, which finished Dundee 1 Hibs 4. Towards the end, jubilant Hibbies taunted their former manager Jim Duffy, by then managing Dundee, by singing 'Duffy, Duffy, what's the score?'

SATURDAY 21st NOVEMBER 1992

A crowd of barely 3,000 braved the snowy weather as Hibs took on Airdrie at Broomfield in the league. A curious choice of tactics by Alex Miller, playing wee Mickey Weir up front with big Keith Wright on the wing, failed miserably, and the Diamonds won 2-0. The most entertaining aspect of this match was the huge snowball fight between the fans on the steep Broomfield terracing.

WEDNESDAY 22nd NOVEMBER 1967

Having already knocked-out Porto in round one, Bob Shankly's Hibees faced off against Italian giants Napoli in the UEFA Cup, second round, first leg, in Naples. 30,000 fans watched the Italians bulldoze Hibs 4-1, Hibs' goal coming from a late Colin Stein strike. Napoli's scorers were Altafini and a hat-trick from Cane. The Hibees were left with what seemed like a mountain to climb in the second leg back in Edinburgh.

WEDNESDAY 22nd NOVEMBER 1972

Eddie Turnbull's men ensured that there would be no all-Glasgow League Cup Final by disposing of Rangers 1-0 at Hampden in front of 47,000 fans. John Brownlie scored the only goal of the game.

SATURDAY 23rd NOVEMBER 2002

Just under 9,000 fans braved freezing weather to see Bobby Williamson's Hibs take on Motherwell at Easter Road in a league match. Terry Butcher's Motherwell were looking for their first win in ten matches, and looked to be on their way to getting it when Steven

Ferguson gave them the lead just after half-time. Motherwell's Sengewald was sent-off after 55 minutes for a second booking, after persistent fouling. Mixu Paatelainen nodded in a Derek Townsley cross three minutes later to draw the Hibees level. The big Finn then turned provider five minutes later, setting up Tom McManus, who headed Hibs into a 2-1 lead. Grant Brebner came on for Hibs with five minutes left and was promptly red-carded just two minutes later, for retaliating to a disgusting challenge by 'Well's Stephen Pearson. Pearson was sent-off for the initial tackle on Brebner as well, as was the Steelmen's David Partridge for getting involved in the confrontation after Pearson's tackle. Eight-man Motherwell eventually lost the match 3-1 to ten-man Hibs, John O'Neil scoring a last minute penalty after he himself had been brought down.

SATURDAY 24th NOVEMBER 1979

Nearly 14,000 fans packed into Love Street, to see hosts St Mirren take on Hibernian in the league. Doug Somner scored twice for the Buddies as they won 2-1, Hibs consolation goal coming in the last minute from a certain George Best, who was making his Hibs debut, and was no doubt the reason for there being such a relatively large crowd. Over 20,000 fans were at Hibs' next game to see Best make his home debut in a 2-1 win over Partick Thistle. Hibs' previous home game, a 1-1 draw with Kilmarnock just two weeks earlier and before the Irishman had been signed, had drawn a crowd of just 5,200, seemingly vindicating Hibernian's decision to sign the talented but troubled forward. Overweight yet still incredibly gifted, Best played just 22 games for Hibernian, scoring three times, yet his skills at times dazzled fans of both Hibs and their opponents, and he initially drew great crowds, home and away. He was unable to save Hibs from relegation, and returned to play in North America after playing a few games at the start of Hibs' 1980/81 division one campaign. Despite his well-documented off the park problems, Best was a football legend, best known for his time at Manchester United, where he won the European Cup in 1968, he also played 37 times for Northern Ireland, scoring nine times.

SATURDAY 25th NOVEMBER 1899

Hibs visited Tynecastle on league business, with Hearts sitting proudly on top of the league. They weren't there at the end of the game as Hibs ran out victors by 3-1 – a margin that could have been more but for the goalkeeping efforts of home custodian Harry Rennie, who of course would later play for the great Hibs teams of 1902 and 1903. Hearts tried to out-muscle their Edinburgh rivals and indeed took an early lead. This did not deter the excellent Hibs team who responded with a hat-trick from the wonderfully named Hamilton Handling. Billy McCartney excelled for Hibs on the left-wing, contrary to many subsequent reports he was not the same person as the future Hibs manager.

SATURDAY 26th NOVEMBER 1955

It had been a rough couple of years for Hibs, but on their day Hugh Shaw's side were more than a match for anyone in the country and this day was one such day as they crushed visitors Partick Thistle at Easter Road by 5-1. Jimmy Mulkerrin, deputising for Lawrie Reilly, opened the scoring for Hibs in the 11th minute, and Willie Ormond added a second on the 17th minute to give Hibs a lead which they held until half-time. After the interval Hibs continued to dominate and further goals came courtesy of the 'sixth member' of the Famous Five Bobby Combe, Willie Ormond again and Eddie Turnbull. Former Hibs player Alex Wright scored a late consolation for the Jags.

TUESDAY 27th NOVEMBER 1962

The second round of the Fairs Cup drew Hibs away for the first leg against Dutch side Utrecht. Hibs won the match 1-0 thanks to an early Duncan Falconer strike, but the other hero of the night was goalie Ronnie Simpson, who saved a second half penalty. Goals from Gerry Baker and Morris Stevenson were enough to win Hibs the second leg in Edinburgh 2-1 on the night, putting Hibs through 3-1 on aggregate.

SATURDAY 28th NOVEMBER 1970

A league match at Brockville watched by just under 8,000 fans saw Willie MacFarlane's Hibs team take on Falkirk. It was MacFarlane's penultimate game in charge of Hibernian and it finished 0-0.

His final game in charge was a 2-0 defeat against Airdrieonians a week later and he was replaced by Dave Ewing. Willie MacFarlane managed Hibs in 57 games, the Cabbage winning 28 of them. His Hibs team scored 105 goals during his reign, conceding 75! As a player at Hibs, in defence, he played 97 times and scored two goals, both of them penalties. He had previously worked in the coal mines before playing for Hibs.

SATURDAY 28th NOVEMBER 1987

During Hibs' league match against Celtic at Easter Road, a member of the now-defunct Celtic Soccer Crew, the Glasgow side's casual group, threw what was thought to have been a tear gas canister/smoke grenade from the Dunbar End onto the East Terrace, home of the hardcore of the Hibs support. The result was panic, as hundreds of choking, terrified fans clambered to escape the fumes, mostly by jumping onto the pitch. Only the small height of the perimeter fencing on the terracing prevented anyone from being crushed or seriously injured. The match had to be paused until the situation was under control and 46 Hibs fans were taken to hospital as a precaution. The grenade in question was believed to have been stolen by the culprit when he was on a Territorial Army exercise on the continent. Celtic won the match 0-1, Frank McAvennie scoring the only goal. Hibs fans had just months earlier had fireworks launched into their 'end' at Ibrox.

WEDNESDAY 29th NOVEMBER 1967

Down 4-1 from the first leg in Naples, Hibernian squared off against Italian giants Napoli at Easter Road in front of 21,000 fans. Bob Shankly's team produced one of the finest Hibs performances ever, to win the second leg of their UEFA Cup second round tie 5-0! Bobby Duncan, Pat Quinn, Peter Cormack, Pat Stanton and Colin Stein all netted for Hibs, who won the famous tie 6-4 on aggregate. Hibs would face England's Leeds United in the next round.

SATURDAY 30th NOVEMBER 1991

McDiarmid Park in Perth was the venue as Alex Miller's men took on St Johnstone in a Premier League match, watched by 6,700 fans. Tommy McIntryre scored the only goal of the game to give Hibs a

1-0 win, nodding in a Joe Tortolano free-kick on 76 minutes, after Saints' defence had failed to clear the ball. Despite the low scoreline, it was a fantastic match, both sides having efforts cleared off the line, both 'keepers making excellent saves and Keith Wright absolutely terrorising the opposing defence. Alex Miller, in the after-match interview, publicly called for Scotland boss Andy Roxburgh to give 'Keef' a chance for the national side, which he eventually did in a friendly against Northern Ireland in 1992.

TUESDAY 30th NOVEMBER 1993

In cold weather and November rain, Hibs played St Johnstone at Easter Road in the league in front of just 5,000 fans. In a game remembered by many Hibbies as simply 'boring and pointless', nothing of any note happened whatsoever, and the dull encounter finished 0-0.

HIBERNIAN FC
On This Day

DECEMBER

SATURDAY 1st DECEMBER 1979

Hibs were in desperate trouble in this season, and the chairman Tom Hart went to the extreme lengths of engaging the services of brilliant but wayward and aging footballer George Best – over the head of his manager, Hibs legend Eddie Turnbull. It was rumoured that Best was paid £2,500 a game, which would be a decent wage in those days. Best had made his debut the previous week at Love Street, but this game marked his home debut and an impressive crowd of 20,622 turned out to see Hibs gain a rare victory. A Partick own-goal and an Ally MacLeod penalty sealed the points, but the result did not see a turnaround and a wretched season ended with Hibs' relegation for the first time since 1931.

SUNDAY 2nd DECEMBER 2012

Hibs faced Hearts in the Scottish Cup fourth round at Easter Road, little more than six months since their 1-5 loss to Hearts in the final of the same competition. This time, Pat Fenlon's men were no pushovers, and won the match 1-0, thanks to a late deflected David Wotherspoon goal. Hibs went on to reach the Final again. In contrast, Hearts were knocked out of the Scottish Cup in December of the NEXT two seasons too, failing to score in humiliating home defeats to Celtic, 0-7 in 2013, 0-4 in 2014.

SATURDAY 3rd DECEMBER 1938

Hibs visited Parkhead, and their young side was on the wrong end of a nine-goal thriller. Willie McCartney had started to mould his team and there had been many positive signs for the Edinburgh side in recent weeks. They struggled against Celtic though, and found themselves 4-2 down early in the second-half when James McLean was forced to leave the field through injury. This was merely the catalyst for an inspired fightback, and a double from Milne to add to the earlier goals from Willie Rice, direct from a free kick, and Tommy McIntyre meant that Hibs had levelled the match at 4-4 going into the closing minutes. Sadly, their efforts were not to yield the point they so richly deserved, when Murphy scored past Hibs goalkeeper James Kerr to steal a 5-4 win for Celtic.

SATURDAY 4th DECEMBER 1943

Cliftonhill hasn't always been the happiest hunting ground for Hibs, but on this occasion they recorded a victory over Albion Rovers in the war time Scottish Southern League. Jimmy Caskie was guesting for Hibs, who were still able to field a strong side. They won by four goals to two, with the goals coming from 19-year-old forwards Gordon Smith and Bobby Combe. Smith, in fact, scored a hat-trick.

SATURDAY 5th DECEMBER 1925

Hibs' strikers were on fire, as they thumped Hamilton Academical by 8-4 in this Scottish League game. Bobby Templeton's side had lost the Scottish Cup Finals of 1923 and 1924 but still retained many of the players from those great sides. Jimmy McColl was on target for Hibs in this game, and he was well on his way to becoming the first player to score 100 league goals for Hibs. Harry Ritchie pitched in with a hat-trick, and future Everton player Jimmy Dunn scored too. George Murray's hat-trick completed the rout.

SATURDAY 6th DECEMBER 1902

A victory at Cappielow moved Hibs nearer the Scottish League title, as it meant they held an eight point gap with just three games to play, although their nearest challengers Rangers had two games in hand. It meant that three points from their remaining three fixtures would be enough to guarantee Hibs the title. Harry Rennie, the Scottish International Hibs goalkeeper was outstanding in his home town, and Hibs sealed the two points for a victory when Bobby Atherton netted after sterling work by Barney Breslin and Jimmy Harrower.

SATURDAY 7th DECEMBER 1946

Willie Ormond made his debut for Hibs as the Edinburgh side visited Palmerston to face Queen of the South, and the teenager marked his debut with a goal as Hibs triumphed by 3-1. Gordon Smith and Willie Peat were also on target. Ormond was to give Hibs outstanding service over the next 15 years, contributing 506 appearances and 189 goals in the green and white jersey. He was also to manage Hibs, taking over from Eddie Turnbull in 1980. Unfortunately, the former St Johnstone, Scotland and Hearts manager was not to manage Hibs for long, as ill health saw him stand down in his first year in the Easter Road hot-seat.

MONDAY 8th DECEMBER 1969

Hibs played a friendly at Easter road against Polish side Gornik Zabrze. Willie MacFarlane's men lost to the Poles 1-2 but this game is best remembered as being the Hibs debut of defender Erich Schaedler, aged 20, who went on to become a club legend. In the game against Gornik, young Schaedler came on as a substitute, eager to win the ball, and accidentally tackled team-mate Peter Cormack, who had to be stretchered off in agony. Schaedler went on to play 434 games in defence for Hibernian in two spells at the club, 1969-1977 and 1981-1985, scoring five times and only being red-carded once. His life ended abruptly and tragically, but he is a true Hibernian legend, nicknamed simply 'Shades'.

WEDNESDAY 9th DECEMBER 1970

Just over 30,000 fans at Easter Road saw Hibs lose the first leg of their third round Fairs Cup/UEFA Cup tie against Liverpool 1-0, John Toshack scoring the only goal of the game.

SATURDAY 9th DECEMBER 1972

A battling performance from Hibs at Hampden Park saw the Hibees win the League Cup Final against Jock Stein's formidable Celtic team. Pat Stanton and Jimmy O'Rourke netted for Hibs, with a young Kenny Dalglish scoring Celtic's consolation. Edinburgh welcomed its heroes back with an open top bus parade. Hibs' boss Eddie Turnbull was as dignified in victory as his counterpart Stein was gracious in defeat.

TUESDAY 10th DECEMBER 1985

John Blackley's Hibernian played Dutch giants Feyenoord in a friendly at Easter Road, in one of many friendlies Hibs played at that time of year back then because the ground had undersoil heating, while other teams' grounds had to cancel matches because of frozen pitches. Hibs easily beat the men from Rotterdam 4-2, the Cabbage's goals coming from a Paul Kane penalty, a brace from Steve 'slim' Cowan' and a strike from Eddie May.

SATURDAY 11th DECEMBER 1993

There were 7,440 fans who braved the elements to venture to Easter Road for Hibernian's league match against Motherwell. The Steelmen missed three great early chances, but Hibs came more and more into the game, and were in the ascendancy at half-time despite going into the dressing room all-square at 0-0. The second-half saw four goals in just 13 minutes, the first coming when Keith Wright headed a Joe Tortolano cross past 'Well 'keeper Sieb Dijkstra. Tommy Coyne grabbed the next two goals, the Ireland striker capitalising on poor Hibs defending to put the Steelmen 2-1 up. The lead didn't last, as Billy Findlay equalised for the Hibees just 50 seconds after Coyne's second goal. The exciting match then saw Motherwell's Miodrag Krivokapic red-carded for fouling Keith Wright, before defender Graham Mitchell headed in a Joe Tortolano corner in the 85th minute, to give Alex Miller's men a 3-2 win.

WEDNESDAY 12th DECEMBER 1962

Jimmy O'Rourke made his debut for Hibernian, in the Fairs Cup second round second leg tie against Utrecht at Easter Road, which Hibs won 2-1. O'Rourke was aged just 16 years and 85 days. He became Hibs' youngest ever scorer just three days later, bagging a goal in a 2-3 defeat by Dunfermline at East End Park. He went on to be one of the finest strikers in Hibs' history, scoring 122 goals in 325 appearances, playing for Hibernian for 12 years! Jimmy also later filled the role of assistant coach to Eddie Turnbull. Unbelievably, O'Rourke was never capped at international level.

SATURDAY 12th DECEMBER 1992

A freezing Easter Road saw Hibs take on Partick Thistle in one of the most tedious matches in living memory. Asides a low, harmless shot from Hibs' Murdo MacLeod, there were no real attempts on goal from open play, Partick Thistle standing up to Hibs in midfield and frustrating Alex Miller's men. In the end, a 0-0 draw was a fair result, except that's not how it finished. Hibs were awarded a soft penalty in the dying minutes, which Darren Jackson duly slammed high into the net past Jags 'keeper Craig Nelson at the Cowshed end. It finished Hibs 1 Partick Thistle 0. Jags boss John Lambie gave a three-word post match interview, saying simply 'we were robbed!'

SATURDAY 13th DECEMBER 1969

Just under 9,000 fans at Easter Road were there to see the Hibees take on Ayr United in the league. Hibs and 'The Honest Men' served up a remarkable seven-goal thriller, all seven goals coming in the first 38 minutes – in a 20 minute spell! Hibernian were never behind, their four goals coming from a brace apiece from Joe McBride and Pat Stanton, Ayr's replies came from Rough and Hood, the latter scoring two.

WEDNESDAY 13th DECEMBER 1978

There were 21,000 fans at neutral Dens Park to see Hibs take on Aberdeen in the League Cup semi-final. Eddie Turnbull's men stubbornly held on until extra-time, when a freak long-range effort from Aberdeen's Stuart Kennedy somehow found its way into the net for the only goal of the game.

SATURDAY 14th DECEMBER 1918

Bottom of the league, Hibs entertained second-bottom Falkirk as both sides looked for a change of luck in this league game. The visitors dominated the game, and well worthy of their 1-0 lead going into the final five minutes. Hibs had rarely threatened, and their forwards were ineffective; only poor finishing from the Falkirk forwards prevented them from sealing the win much earlier. Falkirk were to regret this profligacy, when future Hibs trainer and manager Hugh Shaw scored with a long speculative shot, and better was to follow. In the closing minute Hibs grabbed an unlikely and surprising victory when Willie Robertson scored. The result unfortunately didn't move Hibs off the bottom of the table, though.

SATURDAY 15th DECEMBER 1877

When is a draw not a draw? Well, Hibs met Thornliebank on Scottish Cup business in a fourth-round replay after drawing at their opponents' ground the previous week. Hibs at this time played at Mayfield Park in Newington, which is near the Lady Road area of Edinburgh. This match also ended in a draw after a hard fought contest finished 2-2. Penalty shoot-outs weren't used to settle matches back then, and nor were third replays so both teams advanced to the next round!

SATURDAY 16th DECEMBER 1950

Hibs were in contention for the league title in this year as they welcomed St Mirren to Easter Road. Eddie Turnbull missed out through injury, but Hibs were still too strong for the Paisley side and ran out worthy winners by 3-1. Robert Wood, who deputised for Turnbull, scored one of Hibs' goals, and this was added to by Gordon Smith and by a Willie Ormond penalty.

SATURDAY 17th DECEMBER 1932

Forfar Athletic visited Edinburgh on league business, but were unable to make a dent in the Hibs title charge for the second division. Hibs dominated the game throughout showing that the manager Bobby Templeton had recruited wisely to rebuild the aging team with players who would serve Hibs well in the First Division. Goals from Rob Wallace and James Hart kept the two points in Edinburgh.

THURSDAY 18th DECEMBER 2003

In a re-arranged televised League Cup quarter-final, just under 10,000 fans at Easter Road saw Hibs defeat Celtic to progress to the semi-finals of the competition for the second time in three seasons. Stan Varga gave Celtic the lead but the Hibees, who for once played a physical style of football, equalised through a Grant Brebner penalty, before a late strike by youngster Kevin Thomson sealed the sweet win for Bobby Williamson's men.

SUNDAY 19th DECEMBER 1999

Live on SKY, the final Edinburgh derby of the 20th century was played at Tynecastle, with a 6.05pm kick-off. Hearts had just received a huge investment from SMG and had strengthened their squad. Hibs took an early lead through Dirk Lehmann, and soon doubled the lead with a superb long-range effort by French star Franck Sauzee, who ran all the way from the Gorgie Road end to the opposite end of the ground after the goal, to celebrate with the jubilant Hibbies in the Roseburn Stand. The second-half was exciting, Hibs 'keeper Nick Colgan made some fine saves, but Russell Latapy ran the show. Hibs' young substitute Kenny Miller scored to make it 3-0 late in the second half, giving Hibs a deserved victory. The match has gone down in Hibs folklore simply as 'The Millennium Derby'.

WEDNESDAY 20th DECEMBER 1967

Having already disposed of Porto and Napoli in previous rounds, Elland Road was the venue as Hibs played Leeds Utd in the first leg of their third round Fairs Cup/UEFA Cup match. A crowd of 32,000 saw Leeds win 1-0 thanks to an early Eddie Gray goal. Hibs later had a Colin Stein goal chopped off for no apparent reason.

SATURDAY 21st DECEMBER 1912

Hibs enjoyed a fine victory against Aberdeen at Pittodrie, against a side who had only been formed nine years earlier. Some reports had even suggested their formation was in relation to Hibs' plans to relocate there. Dan McMichael's team were too good for the Dons and goals from Sam Fleming and a double from Willie Smith ensured a comfortable 3-1 victory. Many of the team would go on to contest the Scottish Cup Final in 1914, where they went down to Celtic after a replay.

TUESDAY 22nd DECEMBER 1970

Hibs fans looking for an early Christmas present against Liverpool at Anfield, in their Fairs Cup/UEFA Cup third round second leg match, were disappointed, as Dave Ewing's Hibees lost 2-0 to the Merseyside giants, 3-0 on aggregate. Heighway and Boersma netting for 'Pool, in front of a crowd just short of 40,000.

SATURDAY 23rd DECEMBER 1950

Hugh Shaw's side were well on their way to their second post-war league title when they met Falkirk at Brockville. Christmas shopping didn't entice the 14,000 in attendance, and they witnessed the Famous Five run riot in a 5-1 victory. Archie Buchanan scored, as did Bobby Johnstone, Willie Ormond and Eddie Turnbull with a brace. Hibs finished the day in third place in the table, three points behind leaders Dundee and two behind Aberdeen. As they had four games in hand on Dundee and three games in hand on Aberdeen, they were in an extremely strong position.

SATURDAY 24th DECEMBER 1898

Hibs suffered their record defeat as they crashed 10-0 at Ibrox against Rangers. Despite fielding a strong side and being third in the league table, Hibs were outclassed on this day as the champions Rangers ran riot. In irresistible form, they were five goals to the good before the first half-hour was out, and despite a brief Hibs fightback early in the second-half continued their dominance until the end of the game. Matters could have been worse too, Rangers missed a penalty. However, in the best Ibrox traditions, the referee simply awarded them another one later in the game which was duly converted. The Hibs team, unsurprisingly, looked well beaten before the end.

TUESDAY 25th DECEMBER 1945

Christmas Day was a nightmare for Hibernian as they played a Christmas friendly match against lowly Division B side Dundee at Dens Park. Just over 10,000 fans saw the Dark Blues thump Hibs 4-1, in what was a good natured match, asides from various festive 'missiles' being thrown onto the pitch.

SATURDAY 26th DECEMBER 1981

Bertie Auld's Hibs took on English titans Manchester United in a Boxing Day friendly at Easter Road, Hibs again benefiting from having undersoil heating during the winter freeze that had decimated the British fixtures list. Willie Jamieson gave Hibs the lead, but Manchester United equalised through Frank Stapleton, and an entertaining match in front of a very boisterous crowd ended 1-1.

SATURDAY 26th DECEMBER 1992

Just fewer than 7,000 fans at Brockville were treated to a Boxing Day classic, as Hibs drew 3-3 with Falkirk in a thrilling match, Hibs' goals coming from Gareth Evans and a double by hot youth prospect, David Fellenger.

THURSDAY 26th DECEMBER 2006

A rare boxing-day encounter saw Hearts take on Hibs at Tynecastle, with the Jambos thirsting for revenge after the Easter Road side had knocked them out of the cup a few weeks previously. Hearts turned on the style and went 2-0 up thanks to direct play and some goalkeeping buffoonery by Hibs custodian Zibi Malkowski. Hibs fought back and levelled the match at 2-2, but had Dean Shiels sent-off after some unsportsmanlike play acting by Hearts' Craig Gordon after Shiels had beaten him from the penalty-spot. The thrilling match ended 3-2 to Hearts, Jankauskas, Mikolunas and Hartley scoring for Hearts, while Shiels(pen) and Chris Killen netted for Hibs.

TUESDAY 27th DECEMBER 1960

There were 32,000 fans at Barcelona's Nou Camp for Hibs' UEFA Cup quarter-final 1st Leg against the Catalan giants. Hugh Shaw's Hibees were 2-0 up inside the first 20 minutes through Joe Baker and Johnny Macleod, but Kocsis had Barcelona level at 2-2 after 53 minutes with two fine strikes. Two goals in two minutes from Joe Baker and Tommy Preston had Hibs 4-2 up with just 16 minutes remaining, but the Catalans scored twice in the last seven minutes, Kocsis completing his hat-trick on 83 mins before Evaristo scored a last-gasp equaliser. It finished 4-4, with everything to play for in the second leg in Edinburgh.

MONDAY 27th DECEMBER 1993

Just over 10,000 fans made it to a freezing Easter Road to see Hibernian turn on the style and thrash Partick Thistle 5-1. Hibs' scorers were Hamilton, Wright, Jackson, McAllister and David Farrell, who scored his first goal for the club with a long-range effort. Grant Tierney's stunning second-half overhead kick goal was of scant consolation to the 'Jags. Farrell was later scornfully refused the match-ball by Hibs boss Alex Miller, which he had jokingly asked for on account of his rare goal. With a New-Year Derby looming, this fine display saw Hibs leave the pitch at the final whistle to a chorus of 'Bring on the Jambos' by the fans standing on the East Terrace.

SATURDAY 27th DECEMBER 2014

Rangers hadn't visited Easter Road in just over three years, and since their last visit in December 2011 had gone bust and been liquidated, forming a 'newco' from scratch in 2012, which was admitted to the SPFL's bottom tier. These bizarre circumstances and the relegation of Hibs and Hearts in 2014 saw all three of these big clubs reunited in the Championship. Hibs had already beaten Rangers 3-1 at Ibrox earlier in season 2014/15, and won this second league tie against the 'new' version of the Glasgow side easily, 4-0, with goals from David Gray, Jason Cummings, Scott Robertson and Liam Craig. Hibs fans teased the visiting support by singing 'you're not Rangers anymore', a reference to the club's financial meltdown, but on this day, Rangers were in meltdown on the pitch too. The end of the game saw many Hibs fans stay behind to sing *Sunshine on Leith* in salute to Alan Stubbs and his team.

SATURDAY 28th DECEMBER 1991

A freezing day saw Alex Miller's side 2-0 down to visitors Dundee Utd with just 13 minutes left. Many fans left early, thinking the match over, and they missed a great fightback. Three goals in four minutes from Gareth Evans on 77 and 79 mins and from Keith Wright on 80 mins gave Hibs a 3-2 win. Many Hibs fans only learned about the fightback when they reached the pub or their cars, having left early.

SATURDAY 29th DECEMBER 2001

An Edinburgh Derby at Tynecastle saw Franck Sauzee manage Hibs against Hearts for the first and only time during his ill-fated short spell in charge. Hearts scored early through Kevin McKenna, but battling Hibs snatched a draw with an injury time equaliser from John O'Neil. Sauzee's time as manager was not a great episode in Hibs history, but despite his atrocious record as manager, the big Frenchman preserved his record of never losing to Hearts as player or manager of Hibernian. In the words of the Hibees to their city rivals 'you'll never beat Sauzee'. (Hibs did lose one derby during his time at the club, at the end of season 1999/2000, but Sauzee missed that game through injury, as did Russell Latapy).

SATURDAY 29th DECEMBER 2012

There were 16,800 fans at Easter Road to see Pat Fenlon's men take on champions Celtic in the SPL. Hibernian got off to the perfect start, star striker Leigh Griffiths latching onto a long-ball from Paul Hanlon to skilfully outstrip Celtic's defence and their 'keeper Fraser Forster to score from an incredibly tight angle in front of the away fans, putting Hibs 1-0 up after nine minutes. Hibs were also denied a stonewall penalty when Celtic's Rogne blatantly handled Eoin Doyle's shot in the box. Both sides had plenty of chances and both 'keepers made some great saves, Ben Williams in particular being Hibs' hero in the closing stages. Hibs held on to win the thoroughly entertaining match 1-0.

SATURDAY 30th DECEMBER 1995

Hibs travelled to Ibrox having already beaten the champions there earlier in the season, and looking for a morale boosting result ahead of the coming New Year derby against Hearts. They didn't get it. The Ibrox side humiliated Alex Miller's men 7-0, with ex-Hibs player Gordon Durie scoring four goals. Charlie Miller, Paul Gascoigne and Oleg Salenko completed the rout. Gascoigne was booked during the match for sarcastically 'booking' the referee, as he handed the official his card after he had accidentally dropped it, much to the consternation of both sets of players. Truly a day to forget for Hibs fans, many of whom now dreaded the upcoming game against Hearts.

SATURDAY 31st DECEMBER 1966

Bob Shankly's Hibernian ended 1966 with a victory on Hogmanay against Airdrieonians at Broomfield in the league, in atrocious weather. The Hibees took the lead after 61 minutes when Joe Davies scored a penalty-kick after Jim Scott had been brought down in the box. The Diamonds were unable to reply and the match finished Airdrieonians 0 Hibernian 1, in front of 4,000 freezing fans.

SATURDAY 31st DECEMBER 1994

A rare Hogmanay clash saw Dundee Utd return to Easter Road, where Hibs had already mauled them 5-0 on the opening day of the season. The Arabs were fighting for their lives and looking for a better performance than on their last trip to Leith, which they didn't get. Hibs demolished the Arabs once again, a Keith Wright hat-trick and a goal by Michael O'Neill giving Alex Miller's men another easy win, 4-0.